SIX WORDS

Fresh OFF ★ THE BOAT

LARRY SMITH

SIX WORDS

Fresh OFF ★ THE BOAT

STORIES OF IMMIGRATION, IDENTITY, AND COMING TO AMERICA

BY WRITERS **FAMOUS & OBSCURE**

FROM THE *NEW YORK TIMES* BEST-SELLING **SIX-WORD MEMOIRS SERIES**

EDITED BY **LARRY SMITH**

KINGSWELL

Los Angeles • New York

Due to the sensitive nature of the subject matter in
the current political environment, a handful of names
have been changed at the request of the authors.

For information address Kingswell,
1101 Flower Street, Glendale, California 91201.

Editorial Director: Wendy Lefkon
Executive Editor: Laura Hopper
Cover Design by Shannon Koss

ISBN 978-1-368-00838-9
FAC-020093-17279
Printed in the United States of America
First Hardcover Edition, September 2017
10 9 8 7 6 5 4 3 2

Foreword by

Nahnatchka Khan
& Melvin Mar

I was born in Las Vegas; both my parents were born in Iran. My family was full of characters: dad, mom, grandfather, aunts, uncles, (I remember one uncle telling us all to call him Panther) . . . and they all helped shaped my sense of humor. For me, being a first-generation American, coming from a family of immigrants, it was always important to tell stories from the inside out.

We are telling our story, we are not being told our story. We're not being looked at in a fishbowl, we're looking out at the world through a different lens, with a different perspective. *Fresh Off the Boat* has that same courage. We are confident in who we are, we're not apologizing for it, we're not thankful for it, we own it, we live in it every day. And now is our time to share it. My six words?

We exist because these stories exist.

—Nahnatchka Khan,
creator/executive producer, *Fresh Off the Boat*

My father was the last son to immigrate to America from China. Our family had a long history with this country dating back to the early days of California. They helped build America, but always felt they weren't a part of America. Growing up, my father told me not to make waves. "Keep your head down, do your work, be respectful. You can never go wrong that way."

In many ways, I think my father was right about the realities of surviving in a new country; that was what it was about for his generation. They did the bravest thing: leaving their home to come for a better life for themselves and their family in America, the land of opportunity. Whether it was working on the railroad, to later generations working in Chinatown kitchens or delivering groceries to those same restaurants, they have been an integral part of America. Being the first generation born here, it's my duty to tell our story and participate in making this country a better place. My six words?

I owe it to my father.

—Melvin Mar, executive producer, *Fresh Off the Boat*

This book is inspired by our audience, by viewers across the country, across cultures, and across generations. They tell us that in the story of our television family they see reflections of their own families. That the show could resonate so personally is rewarding; that through this collaboration with Six-Word Memoirs it can also be a catalyst for storytelling is exciting.

In the pages ahead are hundreds of stories. We hope you enjoy them and will kick things off with Six-Word Memoirs from our cast and creative team.

*Designed in Asia,
assembled in California.*

—Ian Chen, "Evan Huang"

**"Where are you *from*?"
I'm Irish-Korean.**

—Kourtney Kang, co-executive producer

Mom's recipes get ruined by me.

—Randall Park, "Louis Huang"

Thanksgiving dinner with samosas and turkey.

—Rachna Fruchbom, coproducer

I learned Hinduism from Urban Outfitters.

—Sanjay Shah, co-executive producer

Still amazed they let me in.

—David Smithyman, executive story editor

我的美国梦想实现了.
My American dream has come true.

—Lucille Soong, "Grandma Huang"

Warning! Land of Opportunity includes "standup."

—Sheng Wang, story editor

Hot pot, free to be me.

—Forrest Wheeler, "Emery Huang"

My family's why I can fly.

—Hudson Yang, "Eddie Huang"

Introduction by
Larry Smith

Grounded in Our Roots, We Rise

As a young boy, I used to love walking down the Atlantic City boardwalk with my grandfather, Morris Smith, whom everyone called "Smitty." Smitty was a small-town pharmacist who immigrated to Philadelphia from Russia in 1914, escaping a war. Just a small boy of four, my grandfather surely didn't realize his family's decision to come to America was a lot like so many other American journey stories, both in its simplicity and in its seriousness: they came hoping for a better life.

My grandfather and I never got very far strolling down the boardwalk. He would inevitably run into someone he knew, and we'd spend the whole time swapping stories with friends, old and new. He talked to everyone. One day it dawned on me that Smitty rarely recounted his early days in America. In fact, I really didn't really know my grandfather's story—a total "fail" for me as a journalist. So I asked him. He was reticent at first: "My story? Who would be interested in that?"

Once he got talking, he didn't want to stop. I not only learned about my grandfather's family history, but I better understood my own place in the world. That's what a good story can do.

Since that day, I've been on a quest to help people tell, share, and seek stories. In 2006, while running a website with Rachel Fershleiser and Tim Barkow, I found that a surprisingly effective way to seek stories was by asking a simple question: Can you describe your life in six words? The prompt was a personal twist on the legend of Ernest Hemingway's six-word story: "For sale: baby shoes, never worn." I saw how wonderful the constraint of six words could be as people responded to this challenge with brief stories that were poignant, memorable, and surprising. Ten years and more than one million six-word stories later, Six-Word Memoirs has become a best-selling book series, a popular lesson plan in classrooms, and a tool for self-expression in environments as varied as churches, therapy groups, weddings, and corporate meetings across the world.

Six Words Fresh Off the Boat: Stories of Immigration, Identity, and Coming to America is the ninth book in the series, and it brings me all the way back to the start as we ask: Who are we as a nation? How does a family's journey to America tell the story of this country as a whole? These questions have been answered, six words at a time, by recent immigrants and refugees, by descendants of the *Mayflower* and those brought by force on slave ships, and by every generation in between. As always, we've invited a handful of celebrities to share their stories, creating a book with a mix of Emmy, Oscar, and Pulitzer Prize winners alongside hundreds of people who have never before been published. And while this project, which asks a timeless question about American identity, was conceived before the election of the forty-fifth president of the United States, the unsettling political climate for immigrants that he has ushered in has made the discussions that follow from these stories more vital than ever.

To gather stories for this book, we put out a call for entries on SixWordMemoirs.com and on our social media channels, as did our collaborators at the acclaimed ABC series *Fresh Off the Boat.* We were invited to work with English-language classes for recent immigrants and refugee organizations across the US. We spent time at naturalization ceremonies and among tour groups at Ellis Island. We put down our smartphones, turned to the people next to us while waiting in lines, and asked one simple question: "What's your story?"

This book is comprised of their answers. The writer and MacArthur "genius" Chimamanda Ngozi Adichie (who shares her own six words on page 203), has spoken on "the danger of the single story." The single story, she says, creates stereotypes, resulting in one story being heard as the *only* story. The six-word form, above all, offers a simple, engaging way to let thousands of stories be told within a limited space. Since each story is just six words—whether written by a Tony winner or a guy named Tony—it's also an egalitarian format that allows many voices to be heard.

Everyone has a story. The sum of our stories is who we are and how we define ourselves as a nation. My grandfather's story—a story of a little boy who escaped Russia with his family during World War I, worked his way through college, opened a small business, became involved in his community, and, ultimately, made life easier for his children—is the American dream. Morris Smith, born Morris Kuznets, came here for a better life. America—at its best—let him.

Larry Smith
June 2017, Columbus, Ohio

Teachers! Educators across the world have found Six Words to be a terrific classroom assignment and catalyst for self-expression. Download our free teacher's guide at sixwordmemoirs.com /fotbguide and engage your students to share their own family stories.

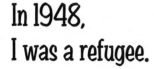

**In 1948,
I was a refugee.**

—The Honorable Madeleine Albright, sixty-fourth US Secretary of State

Welcome,
bienvenue,
bienvenido,
欢 迎,
welkom,
kuwakaribisha.

—Alexandra S. (age 13)

Learning English? Easy.
Learning American: hard.

—Jeff Yang

EVERY IMMIGRANT'S JOURNEY IS TRULY INCREDIBLE.

—Aziz Ansari

Carried few possessions and many dreams.

—Josephine Collett

Wore our flag on his lapel.

—Lynne Marsak Weinberger

Born Hoiping; died NYC WWII vet.

—Michelle Lu for Hank Honghen Hom, US Army Air Forces

Couldn't comprehend America until I left.

—Amanda Palmer

Wisconsin winters: colder than my dreams.

—Neil Gaiman

TRAVELING BEFORE there wAs A Border.

—Billy Collins

We stayed because of First Amendment.

—Molly Jatta

Traded rationed
candy for
banned books.

—Richard Chen

From Russia, via Israel, with lox.

—Leonid Oliker

Thank you for standing with humanity.

—Emanuel Solomon

We've always been here.
Blackfeet Nation.

—Michelle Lowe

Open border via
Aguascalientes for steel.

—Ida Sandoval

Bottom of the boat as cargo.

—Takiyah Nur Amin

I migrated to live
openly gay.

—XinFeng Lin

Saïd Sayrafiezadeh is not
an immigrant.

—Saïd Sayrafiezadeh

First Things First: Find a Bicycle
By Lac Su

Our family immigrated to Hollywood, California, in 1978 as Vietnamese refugees. We left everything behind; my parents' wedding rings were the only valuables to make it out with us. My father knew we could adapt to a new life in America with what little we had. With hard work, the possibilities are endless. But . . . first things first. He needed a bicycle to get around until he learned enough English to pass the driver's license test.

Before enrolling my sister and me in school, my father searched local Dumpsters looking for enough bicycle parts to build a complete bike. Within weeks, he found what he needed— even inner tubes that he patched and reused. For a few years, that red ten-speed bicycle was his prized possession. While other refugees did what they could to get their feet wet in America, my father was already getting his bicycle tires wet—peddling to and from work every day, rain or shine. When the sun was out, I rode with him. He placed me on the bicycle frame in front of him and

With hard work, the possibilities are endless.

took me on errands. We went to the liquor store to get cigarettes or pay the utility bills, and if I was lucky, to the grocery store.

One time on his way home from work he decided to explore Los Angeles. He got lost. He didn't read or speak English. He couldn't find his regular route back home—a route that he'd been taking repeatedly for a year. He left work at 6:00 p.m. and didn't get home until the next morning at 9:00 a.m. His explanation to my mother: "Every street and every building in downtown L.A. looked the same. I thought I could remember the landmarks instead of street names, but after a few miles, all the buildings began to look the same."

After a few years of saving, my father bought his first American car—a red 1976 Chevrolet Chevette. Though he passed the driver's license test and could drive around, he didn't. The red car was covered with cloth to protect the paint from the blazing Southern California sun. It was too expensive and beloved to take out regularly. Instead, he continued to ride his bicycle everywhere until it was time to teach me to ride. His red ten-speed soon became mine. Like my father, I learned the ins and outs of the Los Angeles streets by getting lost. Many times.

There was something about riding around L.A. that made me fall in love with America. The most important thing I learned on these rides: despite all the different people and cultures in Los Angeles, we had one promising thing in common. We were all trying to chase the American dream—one block at a time.

Lac Su is the author of the award-winning memoir, I Love Yous Are for White People.

JUST YOUR AVERAGE MEXICAN-AMERICAN JEWISH-ITALIAN MAYOR.

—Los Angeles Mayor Eric Garcetti

ANOTHER GREEK ODYSSEY, THRIVING IN AMERICA.

—Arianna Huffington

Will Always Be Daughter Number Three
By Maw Shein Win

My parents emigrated from Burma to the United States in the early sixties. I was the first child born in the US, but the third in the family. It is common in Burmese culture to refer to one's children by their birth order. To this day, my mother still introduces me as Daughter Number Three. Both of my parents were doctors. Now my mother, Ayya Gunasari, is a *bhikkhuni* and has a monastery in Joshua Tree, California. And Daughter Number Three? She's first poet laureate of El Cerrito, California.

Maw Shein Win is a poet, editor, and educator who lives and works in the Bay Area.

Emerged, educated, emigrated, immigrated. Elected. Elated.
—Adam Killeya

Kimchi to lutefisk via Flying Tiger.
—Deborah Johnson

Two homes
opposite sides of the world.

— Daphne Eleftheriadou (age 15)

Thailand's crazy boy,
America's analytical man.

—Yiem Sunbhanich

FROM CAR TRUNKS TO CITY LIGHTS,

—Imogene C.

I can't find sambal bajak anywhere.

—Tammy Manse

Scottish estate daughter
elopes with gardener.

—Amy McKenzie

Third generation, now considering a return.

—Michael Finkel

I'm not angry I'm just Pakhtun.

—Khadija B. (age 16)

Wonder slice in pan dulce loaf.

—Liz Shannon

Iranian immigrant breaking barriers in Hollywood.

—Shohreh Aghdashloo

Moving forward is what immigrants do.

—Lisa Qiu

Written by:
Tanzila Ahmed

Art by:
Fahmida Azim
(Ingredients:
sugar, spice, and
righteous fury.)

In mother's belly, I crossed borders.
Anchor baby, fresh off the boat.
Born here, but never feeling here.
Daughter of Bengal Third World refugee.
Gold paved streets are enticing traps.
Au contraire, bacon isn't Muslim kryptonite.
Inshallah, don't kick me off flight.
My America, perpetually second-class citizen.
Modern-day Western: Cowboys vs. Immigrants.

It's not a "tan." It's melanin.
India's partition was Nana's "Muslim Ban".
Muscle memory reminds me to survive.

I dream in poetry and rage.

Tiny Syrian, too American,
never enough.

—Rayya Elias

ARRANGED MARRIAGE BROUGHT ME TO FREEDOM.

—Tahira Bhatti

Armenian grandparents: when refugees were welcome.

—Bernard Ohanian

My mother: maid to mechanical engineer.

—Jennifer Na

Zeiger too ethnic! How about King?

—Larry King

"They Are Coming to Kill You"

By Walid Ali

Photo by Tariq Mohamed

I was twenty-nine, just married, and living in my home country of Iraq during the time of the fallen regime in 2004. I had a good job working as an interpreter for the United States Army, which at that time was helping to rebuild Iraq.

Then my name ended up on a list. This list, which I believe was run by a terrorist group, accused me of being a traitor. The list claimed that I was a spy working for the United States Army. If those in charge of the list saw me, they would need to kill me. That's what happens if you're on a list.

Another interpreter I knew was bombed. Three days later, more interpreters who were on that list were killed. At the time, my wife and I were living with my mom. One morning, Mom woke up to find something outside of our house that looked like a big can of milk. The mixture in the can was actually a handmade bomb, but we didn't know that at the time. The police came and explained that something had gone wrong with the electrical part of the bomb. We were lucky. And I have seen death many times with my own eyes.

In the weeks after, I tried to go about life as usual. One day, I took a taxi to a barbershop. Everyone in the barbershop kept looking at me. Then someone rushed toward me and said, "What are you doing here? They are coming to kill you right now." I thought no one had recognized me. The man persisted and told me I needed to run. I left the barbershop without a haircut, called my wife, and said, "We need to leave Iraq today." She was carrying our first child at the time.

We left for Yemen and went straight to the United Nations office. I explained what happened and registered myself as a refugee. I was given temporary refugee protection documents. Then I waited. From 2004 to 2008 I resided in Yemen, teaching English. For four years I heard no news about getting out of the country. Not a single call. I went back to the office in 2008 and asked for help  again. At first I was denied entry to the office. They said I needed an appointment. No one was giving me an appointment. I really didn't know what to do. Then a stranger, an old man, saw what was going on and spoke to a security guard. Some-how, what he said worked. When the lady at the desk heard my story, she said I should have been resettled a long time ago.

I waited eight more months for the security check. Finally, a call came. I was told to be at the airport in fifteen days. I didn't know where we were flying to until we got to the airport. They gave my wife, my three-year-old daughter, and me boarding tickets that read COLUMBUS, OHIO. I had never heard of this place.

I came to the United States with $300 in my pocket, not knowing what to do or where to start. But with the help of a local church and a refugee services organization called CRIS, my family was given a place to live and food to eat.

Eight years later, I am a completely different person from the one who landed at the airport. We have adapted well to a totally different country. But adaptation is hard. Many first-generation refugees will suffer from a loss of identity throughout their lives. Being uprooted from your country is just like trying to uproot a tree. When you plant a tree, it grows roots so deeply into the ground that it's damaging if you pull the tree out, remove the roots, and try to plant it elsewhere. The tree will never be the same.

Now I run a small construction business. Helping to build and repair homes in America gives me great joy. I have many friends. My kids are getting a very good education and speak both English and Arabic. We have a very good life in the United States.

Are there bad people from my community? Yes. But do they represent everyone? No. The majority of the people in refugee communities are very nice people. They are peaceful. They are grateful to the country that has let them come in. They feel lucky. We want to pay back the country that allowed us to start over.

Walid Ali, an American citizen, owns a construction business in Ohio.

A HYPHENATED,
CAFFEINATED,
AMERICAN
FROM KAZAKHSTAN.

—Akbar Mamatkhanov

AMERICA WAS OUTSIDE
OF MY IMAGINATION.

—Nuna Sharma (age 16)

**Why did I escape?
They didn't.**

—Obse Ababiya

Tired. Poor.
Huddled masses.
Seeking hope.

—Ken Stasiak

**Austria between wars.
Texas was safer.**

—Meredith Hefner

**She homesteaded;
he skied in supplies.**

—Stacy Mueller

Germany: escaped.
England: survived.
America: lived.

—Zack Kardon

"Are you related to Bruce Lee?"

—Karen Lee

A secret life because of immigration.

—Kimberly G. (age 11)

Escaped from death; now we hide.

—Anderson A. (age 17)

New wall, new ways to arrive.

—Oscar Andres Perez (age 17)

So many types of milk products!

—Vladimir Goldstern

"WHERE ARE YOU REALLY FROM?" HERE.

—Alyssa Nitta

We immigrants are America's true superpower.

—Junot Díaz

Germany destroyed family.
America rebuilt it.

—Ari Wallach

BROKEN TAILLIGHT, FLASHING LIGHTS.
"WHERE'S DAD?"

—Juan J. Martinez-Hill

My Dutch dad breezes through customs.

—Charlie Stuip

Ordering coffee at Starbucks
is complicated.

—Priya Ramanathan

Born in Tule Lake.
Google it.

—Kouji Nakata

"Welcome": A Powerful Force for Good

By Kitti Murray

Photo by Manuela Montañez Guerra

Leon Ndahimwa Shombana calls himself the "firstborn" at Refuge Coffee, a nonprofit started in 2015 to bring together recent immigrants and locals in our community in Clarkston, Georgia. The majority of new immigrants have never been inside an American home. Since the coffee shop is an extension of American living rooms and offices—places where people come to work or mingle—it's an ideal place to bridge that gap.

All of our baristas are refugees and immigrants, transitioning from survival mode to building a life here. Leon began as a test case for our mission, and now he's something like a lead investigator. He was the first to benefit from the mission and adopt it as his own, the first to share it with our neighbors and beyond. That mission is stamped on our coffee sleeves and emblazoned on our trucks:

As you enjoy this drink,
you are providing a living wage,
quality job training, and mentorship
for a refugee who lives right here
in Atlanta's own backyard.

Every day, we roll out a welcome mat in the heart of Clarkston, a little city on the outskirts of Atlanta that *Time* magazine called "the most diverse square mile in the country." Our welcome mat is a makeshift coffee shop in a garage. For the past year, Leon has greeted customers from close to seventy-five countries. He's served espresso and hibiscus tea alongside our other trainees from Syria, Ethiopia, Burma, Central African Republic, and Morocco.

We use words like, "How may I help you?" and "Have a seat," and "Where are you from?" In these dignified exchanges, which are both friendly and professional, our employees learn to personalize American hospitality, and in turn, they open people's eyes to the vibrancy and resilience of most refugees.

Leon was a history teacher in his home country of Democratic Republic of the Congo, and he'd like to teach again one day. For now, he is teaching about the good that is inherent in welcoming, from the smallest child, who makes chalk drawings on our patio, to the biggest celebrity, who hires the truck to treat her cast and crew on set. He's teaching us that "welcome" is a simple word but an essential way of treating each other. "Welcome" is a powerful force for good.

Kitti Murray is the founder of Refuge Coffee Co., a nonprofit collaborative that employs refugees, offering them a living wage and professional training in the diverse community of Clarkston, Georgia.

Clarkston: Ellis Island of the South.

–Clarkston, Georgia Mayor Ted Terry, who explains that with more than sixty languages spoken in this 1.4-square-mile city, it is home to longtime Georgians living side by side with recent immigrants and refugees.

Her first language,
no speakers left.

—Melesha Owen

Buried his accent,
buried his identity.

—Amy Nealon

I WAS PROUD
TO DEFEND AMERICA.

—Hassan Al Nuaimi

New arrivals
become the next hosts.

—Chip Beck

Oldest sibling,
only one with accent.

—Alberto Gonzalez

AMERICA, THANKS FOR ADOPTING MY FAMILY.

—Regina Spektor

AND SUDDENLY WE WERE ALL AMERICANS.

—Jack Dishel

Twenty dollars and just one suitcase.

—Jessica Lauchaire

Immigrant → National Medal of Arts winner.

—Moises Kaufman

We came,
we saw,
we stayed.

—Viet Thanh Nguyen

1608: my family;
1992: my husband.

—Catherine P. Cua

FROM ENGLAND, 1877,
FIREFIGHTER IN CHICAGO.

—Brian Ellis

Mom left Franco's Spain for hope.

—Cristina Breshears

One "sauce" nana, one "gravy" nana.

—Cheryl Della Pietra

Sold *Schmattas* to the Gold Miners

By Susan Uran Evind

On the Jewish side of my family, my great-great grandmother and her daughter—my great-grandmother—emigrated from Czechoslovakia to San Francisco. They set up shop along the wharf to sell clothing to prospectors during the California gold rush. They did fine, but their clothing stand wasn't as prosperous as that little guy's shop next door to theirs. His name was Levi Strauss.

Susan Uran Evind is a voice-over artist and a third-generation Californian with ancestors who came from everywhere else.

EUROPEAN JEWS
TURN RAGS
INTO RICHES.

—Steve Shapiro

We were sold to mine owners.

—Dan Akers

HUGUENOTS CHOSE RELIGIOUS FREEDOM
OVER DEATH.

—Jill Vickers

"Nonconformists" asked
to leave England, 1600s.

—Hunter Moon

Kicked out everywhere: religion,
revolution, highlanders.

—Amy McKee

PRUSSIAN MILITARY CONSCRIPTION:
no THANK you.

—Holly Hartman

I'm an All-American mongrel. You?

—Piper Kerman

I NO LONGER NEEDED
TO WHISPER.

—Hanni Gorenz Finaro

Polish spirit.
Anne, Anna,
then Ana.

—Ana Shinal

Adding new shades
to comedy, satire.

—Hasan Minhaj

Learned all English
and still foreign.

—Beau Sia

Ice Falling from Sky Sounded Magical

By Nari Ward

Photo courtesy of the artist and Lehmann Maupin,
New York and Hong Kong.

I moved to the United States from Jamaica when I was twelve. My mother had made a home for our family in New York City a few years earlier and was bringing each of the kids over one at a time.

My father joined us last. He didn't want to leave the Caribbean, but neighbors convinced him that he would have an amazing experience in America.

They talked of "ice falling from the sky." That sounded magical, especially in the tropics, where ice was this thing that somebody would bring over in a cart. I was really intrigued with this kind of magical possibility: that you could make a man, a snowman, out of ice. One of my sculptures is comprised of dried mango pits in the shape of snowmen.

I became a naturalized citizen in 2012 and have since felt freer to make political art. Whether it's about police brutality, power structures, or community disempowerment, my work explores the experiences of immigrants and issues relevant to communities of color.

Nari Ward is the 2017 winner of the Vilcek Prize in Fine Arts, recognizing immigrant artists who make a contribution to US culture through their art. His works have been exhibited across the world, including at the Whitney Biennial in 2006, and he has received commissions from the United Nations and the World Health Organization, among others.

Hinda became "Helen."
God bless America.

—Sally Friedman

I wore the wrong shirt.
Always.

—Gary Shteyngart

Passport progression:
pierogies, parmigiano,
poutine, pizza.

—David Linetsky

Globe-trotting Venezuelan diplomat
anchors in Ohio.

—Fernando Rincon

Parents Indian, found tuna casserole exotic.

—Madhu Dahiya

MORE ASSIMILATED THAN A BAGEL BLT.

—Joel Levinson

Now in America,
I become Black.

—Naki Akrobettoe

My father's Mandarin: always an impersonation.

—Addie Tsai

Not from Here, Not from There

By Lorenzo Hernandez

After so many years of being away, I finally come back home. My *pueblo* rests in between the mountains. The houses are tan and square, the roads are just dirt. My feet kick the dust up high as I run toward my grandma. As I pass by houses, avoiding stepping on the chickens, people shout and wave to me. The village is so small—everybody recognizes who I am. There is a group of people outside, sitting on crates, laughing. I ask them if they know where my abuelita is. They point me farther ahead.

Eventually, I get tired of searching, so I relax at the library. I'm looking through a book when someone calls out to me. I turn to see who it is. A woman in a black dress with a colorful serape draped across her shoulders and a long braid with strands of gray asks me, *"Quieres ver tu abuelita?"* Yes! Oh, yes, I want to see her so badly. The old lady takes me to my mother's childhood home. There is no door and I raise my leg when I enter, so I don't trip on the elevated floor. Surprise! All my tios and tias are there. I greet everybody. The room is lit with warmth and laughter. I am home.

If only my dream could become a reality. Up until a few months ago, I was an undocumented immigrant. I was two and half years old when I shared a car with a family of strangers with forged documents and crossed the border into the United States. A few years later, my mother finally reunited with my father here in the States. I have no memories of my own of Mexico. My parents' stories are how I understand where we come from.

Growing up, being undocumented did not mean much. It just meant that I was invisible to the system. It wasn't until I grew older that I found out what it meant. It meant I couldn't get a job, apply for a license, or get an ID. When I learned all of this, I vowed to not let those restrictions stop me from doing what I wanted. Sure, I couldn't get a bank account; so I'd just sign the check with my father's name. If there was a section to write my social security number, could I skip it? Yes, I could. We find loopholes to get by.

> Growing up, being undocumented meant I was invisible to the system.

In 2014, I heard about DACA. I stared at the desktop screen in amazement as I learned of the benefits. What is it exactly, though? Short for Deferred Action for Childhood Arrivals, it's a policy created by President Obama in August 2012 allowing undocumented children who came to this country at an early age to obtain a social security number to use for employment. It also offers protection from deportation. Some of DACA's requirements for applicants: no criminal record of more than one misdemeanor; migration to the United States before sixteenth birthday; obtain an education. There are more than one million undocumented immigrants in this country eligible to apply for DACA. Of those people, approximately 750,000 are DACA recipients, also known as "DREAMers" (Development, Relief, and Education for Alien Minors/DREAM Act).

A few months after I turned fifteen, I began preparing to apply for DACA. I obtained assistance from an advocate in Oakland, California, to help me apply. My advocate led us through the whole process. I had to gather evidence to prove I had been in the United States every month since 2007. My evidence consisted of attendance certificates, semester grades, and letters from my teachers. A few weeks later a noticed arrived. I was instructed to get my fingerprints taken.

It took less than five minutes for the man to take fingerprints of all ten of my fingers. One thought kept circling inside my brain: I exist! I exist to them now! I'm not invisible! A few months later I received my social security number. These nine characters—mine!—meant I could finally open a bank account and apply for the paid internship I had been waiting a year for. However, even with my DACA status, it is still highly unlikely I will ever visit Mexico. There are only three reasons

I can leave the country: for a sick family member or emergency family matter, for an educational reason, or for an employment purpose. Then I'd have to pay a $575 fee to apply for what's called "advanced parole."

Whenever anyone asks me where I want to go in the world, I always say Mexico. I'm often greeted with looks of confusion. Why would I want to go there? Because that's where my family is, where a whole part of my life is missing. I'm a DREAMer, asleep and awake.

I dream of my parents being able to visit Mexico to see all their brothers, sisters, parents, and friends. I dream of being able to know all of them. I dream that all of us—the undocumented—will be able to reunite with those we left behind.

Lorenzo Hernandez was born in Guadalajara, Mexico, and raised in Hayward, California.

DREAMers are only allowed to dream.

—Ivy Teng Lei

Ethiopian jazz and injera
in Brooklyn.

—David Hunegnaw

SIX people in trunk,
five hours.

—Carlos B. (age 17)

Thankful for Pakistani
adoption law loopholes.

—Alia Zareen Garvey

Don't know which one is home.

—Francesca Zipser (age 15)

Dad, Oklahoma's first
Asian school principal.

—Sharon Hsieh for Dick Hsieh

Four little girls
without their parents.

—Kurt Amann

*Dad was "coyoted" here
from Guatemala.*

—Michael Mares

Mom by desert,
kids by plane.

—Esmerelda A. (age 17)

Papi came
looking for his querida.

—Nora Guadalajara

Wife on train, husband follows tracks.

—John Charlton

Quick Freedom Flight. Couldn't Finish Coke.

By Lydia Martin

Photo courtesy of Lydia Martin

I was six in 1970 when my mother and I left Cuba aboard a Freedom Flight, part of a program that delivered about three hundred thousand Cuban refugees to the United States between 1965 and 1973. My mother had vowed to escape Fidel Castro's bloody, oppressive regime at any cost. She gave up her homeland, her family, her friends. She also gave up the love of her life, the man she married seven months before she was suddenly given government permission to leave the island (she had divorced my father when I was three).

In her late twenties and faced with an agonizing choice, my mom decided her priority was to ensure that I'd grow up in the land of liberty. She didn't see her husband again for more than forty years. They reunited in Miami in their late sixties, when Cuba finally allowed him to leave. But they learned there is no reclaiming the past.

I remember very little about that actual flight to freedom— Varadero to Miami in about fifty-two minutes—but I do remember a flight attendant serving me a cold Coca-Cola. My very first. I was hooked for life. And I remember her taking it away, only half finished, when it was time to land in Miami.

Lydia Martin is a fiction writer and columnist for the Miami Herald.

But where are you *really* from?

—Suki Kim

Ninety miles and one world away.

—Roberto Jiménez

Welcome, my newly mispronounced last name.

—Lena Bridonneau (age 15)

Pale of Settlement ⟶ Tan of Boca.

—David Wolkin

Despite adversity, reached the Promised Land.

—Clara Hart

She said she was from Babylon.

—Jasmine Kirschbloom

Immigrants Can Be Just as Patriotic

By Dr. Gulshan Harjee

Although I have lived in four countries and have seen and experienced many regimes—dictatorship, communism, socialism, democracy—I call America home. The United States is the greatest nation in the world: it is the kindest and most compassionate, and regardless of political climate, those values will not change.

My grandparents, from India, were taken to East Africa—where my parents were born—to help the Germans build the East African railway. I was born in Tanzania. During my high school years, Idi Amin was expelling Asians from Uganda—Asians who had lived in East Africa for a couple of generations—an idea moving south to Tanzania. My father made the very difficult decision to let me go to Pakistan to finish high school. I was about to start medical school in Pakistan when the war broke out with India. Again, I had to leave.

Still with a Tanzanian passport, I went to Iran. I had never spoken a word of Farsi, so I spent the first six months learning that language, and then I started college. Two years into medical school, I had to leave again. I had been able to get a scholarship from Iran's queen, Farah Pahlavi, to finish medical school; however, the schools were closed during the Iranian embargo, and the shah and empress of Iran went into exile. So I came to the United States.

I had only six months left on my Tanzanian passport until I would become stateless. I got very lucky—I was able to get a student visa and attended Morehouse School of Medicine, which at the time was a two-year school. I then transferred to Emory and got my MD. While doing my residency, I had the fortunate opportunity to apply for my green card because my residency was in an underserved area. I am proud to have started a primary care practice in Decatur, Georgia: a practice with twenty-four employees, where we speak fifteen languages and accept all forms of insurance.

It was heartbreaking to see that refugees come here, get six months of Medicaid, then many must do without health care. With the help of an interfaith board and a friend who is a pharmacist, we put together the Clarkston Community Health Center. Free of charge, we provide primary care, dental, mental health, and prescriptions for people who qualify—almost everyone who walks through our doors. In just two years, we have built a roster of about two thousand patients. Every person who works there is a volunteer; about 80 percent of those volunteers are of immigrant backgrounds. Most of us were not born here—giving back is how we show our patriotism to this country. Immigrants, we are contributing, meaningful citizens.

Dr. Gulshan Harjee is a native of Tanzania. She speaks six languages and has been displaced many times due to persecution and war.

Photo courtesy of Dave Stewart

I witnessed it: Delta Blues. Sacrosanct.

—Dave Stewart

Three people, six years, finally safe.
—Alen Hodzic (age 13)

Refugees aren't burdens, they are investments.
—Heval Mohamed Kelli

Slovenia is not Slovakia.
Nor Russia.
—Anze Kopitar

Born African. Raised American.
Speak Hindi.
—Janiah Smith (age 12)

Immigrant son proudly
dresses First Lady.
—Narciso Rodriguez

F1, H1B, green card, blue passport.

—Maud Brillet

Claimed accountant profession;
later became one.

—Virginia Pasley

CAME FROM WALES
TO DIG COAL.

—Todd Evans

Italian stonecutter who
came to build.

—Alice Brach DiLaura

Rushed moving van
before visa expired.

—Joel Walsh

My accent has become my voice.

—M. Night Shyamalan

Is there fish sauce in Nebraska?

—Thakoon Panichgul

MERIT DIDN'T GRANT VISA,
LOVE DID.

—Andrea Jimenez Mudafar

SAN Francisco needed
More Scots GARdeners.

—Katherine Pitta

Irish-German mash:
potato eaters united.

—Ann McGlinn

Traded Russian shtetl
for Bronx tenement.

—Lori Dorn

Oppression became opportunity; poverty became prosperity.

—Louise Hopewell

FORTY YEARS LATER: STILL OUTSIDE IN.

—Derek Kei Lap Cheng

HERE WHEN IT WAS STILL MEXICO.

—Audrey Madisōn

Limited English vocabulary, so Dad improvised.

—Amy Lee

I will crush the bamboo ceiling.

—Tiina Naksu

Love from Beirut, Lebanon, to Columbus

As told to Zaynah Ahmed by the mother and children of the Alshahal family (Mother: Randa. Children: Ali, Ismail, Abed, Nohal, and Manal)

From war-torn Beirut to the burgeoning city of Columbus, Ohio, the Alshahal family is an "American dream" story. Arriving in the United States with just a few hundred dollars, "Baba" Kamal Ali Alshahal worked long hours, eventually opening up his own supermarket. Two decades later, his children run the A&R Creative Group in Columbus, Ohio, a collection of farm-to-table restaurants and breweries, each different in style, yet all linked by the community values instilled by their parents. Around a large communal table at one of their restaurants, the family shared the story of their remarkable journey

ALI: We were a middle-class family, born and raised in Beirut, Lebanon. When civil war broke out in 1986, the fighting got close to us and we were hit by a bomb. Some family members passed away; some of us were injured. My father found a way to save us himself. He was standing outside when it happened, went inside the bank, and literally was the ambulance driver—Father was a paramedic—and he saved our lives. Our father stayed in the hospital with us for nine months; he stayed in contact with some of his friends. He had a Hungarian ambassador friend who was able to get us a visa to come to the US.

Photo courtesy of Alshahal family

RANDA: Abed, my youngest son, had not yet been born, but my husband and my first four children and I arrived in the United States. We went from Pennsylvania to Columbus to stay with my brother and realized there was a future here—a place we could settle our roots and allow them to grow. We came with just $1,000. We paid $800 for a car and $200 was left. We were forced to leave everything behind. That was the hardest part. My husband [who passed away in 2015 from cancer] was such a strong man; but when we first arrived here, most nights I would watch him cry.

ALI: We didn't feel resentment about being moved to America; it was more of a resentment for the situation: Why us? Where are our friends? Where is our culture? There was almost resentment for Lebanon itself: Why did it do that to us? In Lebanon our father was a paramedic, a job he loved, but he had to find a different job in the US. Here his work was simply a means to an end, and that end was to support our family.

MANAL: We grew up knowing our home was between Lebanon and Columbus; we felt both were equally ours, we identified with both. We would look forward to our summers spent in Lebanon, and we still take our children there every year to make sure they not only know where their roots are from, but so they have a sense of ownership of Lebanon and America.

ISMAIL: Our father worked at a convenience store. He was such a hardworking guy the owner of the store offered to go into business together. He trusted his work ethic so much he offered him a partnership in the store. Baba didn't only want to make money; he wanted to make friends. He wasn't passionate about selling chips or cigarettes. He was passionate about what that represented. His biggest strength was his heart.

NOHAL: A similar vibe runs through our restaurants. I think growing up, we all understood the importance of community and culture and maintaining these tight-knit relationships. The business blossomed and grew from each sibling's contribution, just as they did in our homes.

ISMAIL: I was in Iraq working for the State Department when Ali called me and said, "Let's bring you back home so you can be with the family." I came back from Iraq and drove down and stopped right in front of Fourth Street Patio, which would become our first restaurant. As soon as that happened, it was a no-brainer. I got out, finished my contract, and came home.

ALI: America is our home, but our father left us our roots in Lebanon, made sure we visited, whether we liked it or not. We are Lebanese-American; we are just as American as we are Lebanese. Our friends always came over to our house. It was a place our two cultures united.

SIX WORDS

62

As a family we rarely went out to eat. And I remember we all really wanted to go to KFC, a very American establishment. Finally our dad took us there . . . and brought pita bread with him to go with the chicken! Our Lebanese culture was always with us.

ABED: As hard as the struggle was, and as poor as we were, our parents never made us feel in any way, shape, or form that we were barely getting by. Our father worked twenty hours a day and my mother worked part-time. Going out to eat was a very, very special occasion; the movies were always the dollar theater. We were fortunate enough to have family and friends to support us, strangers both to befriend us and teach how to utilize the resources around us. We were a middle-class family in Lebanon turned poor refugees in America, yet as children we hardly felt the difference.

> **Father's last advice: Please stay together.**

ALI: My favorite story about our father is the Nintendo story. We had just purchased a video game console—Super Nintendo! Sometimes he would call from the store at the time when we were supposed to be doing homework and ask, "Are you guys playing Nintendo?" We'd have it on mute and start lying about it and he would say, "I already know." Then we would admit it and say, "Yes, Dad. I'm sorry." He'd given us strikes; we had many strikes. He said, "The next time I'm going to break it."

ABED: One afternoon Baba had called and I answered the phone. He asked, "What are your brothers doing?" I was a little kid, so I said, "Oh, they're just playing video games." He locked up the store, closed up during open hours, came and stomped on it, walked out, and went back and opened the store again.

NOHAL: Both our parents wanted to have strong, independent, well-rounded children; I think that's what allowed us to thrive. Our father was strict, yet generous—and always a man who stayed true to his word.

ALI & ABED: Before our father died, his last advice was, "Please stay together." And so we do. Every Sunday, well over twenty of us come together at our childhood home and gather around the table to eat, talk, share, and just be together. We realize the importance of that throughout all of our restaurants and we want to take a piece of that and try to make it go even deeper for our customers. Our father's behind-the-scenes advice to our family was: "When you leave this world, how much wealth you will carry with you will come from the good things people say about you, and your name itself." According to his own words, our father died quite a wealthy man.

We all have traditional Muslim names.

—Gabourey Sidibe

Delivering homemade dumplings in Bryant Park.

—Binfei Lai

THEN: GRANDMA'S TORTILLAS. NOW: RESTAURANT TORTILLAS.

—Jasson Enriquez (age 17)

''Filipino? Oh! I've had lumpia before!''

—Christine Espiritu

Your dad's in the navy, too?

—E. Ignacio

My mother: "Salamat."
Me: "You're welcome."

—Arvin Temkar

A Father Swims, a Daughter Soars
Wai Chim

My father began his journey to America as a poor man escaping from a poverty-stricken village in Mao Zedong's China. In search of a better life, he dove into shark-infested waters to make the long grueling swim to the then British colony of Hong Kong, and finally to the US.

I am immensely humbled by this great man and his brave act that has allowed me to enjoy a beautiful life, to go to college, to travel and work in exciting industries, and, ultimately, to write my first book for young adults, one based on my father's story.

Wai Chim is a children's author from New York, currently based in Sydney, Australia.

Chinese refugee swims to American citizenship.
—Chris Cheng

ABANDONED THE PIANO FOR A BASKETBALL.
—Jeremy Lin

"We came for you. Do well."

—Knoa Tsang Jaffe

PROPOSAL? IMMIGRATION LAWYER SAID "GET MARRIED."

—Dory Thrasher

Dosvedanya, Gorbie.
Hello, Ronnie. Deep breath.

—Ilya Perchikovsky

Mexican blood but can't speak Spanish.

—Marcelia Nava

About. I said about. Not a-boot.

—Drew Doughty

Mom left Scotland at ten. Forever.

—Julianne Moore

Texas was Mexico.
Border crossed us.

—Maria Dolores Castillo

How do I become
"just American"?

—George Tri Nguyen

Jesus who's not from the sky.

—Jesus Mendoza (age 17)

My name is not *mamacita,*
okay?

—Dori N. (age 17)

MOM LEFT JAPAN:
1959. NEVER RETURNED.

—Bill Bonk

**Another immigration;
must run in blood.**

—Sara Abou Rashed

**Despite objections, Marine
marries Japanese host.**

—Ron McGhee

Ran from Nazis; we're not Jewish.

—Eva Fiedler (age 15)

**RWANDA TO AMERICA,
AGE FIFTEEN, ALONE.**

—William Hamlin

**Champion fighter:
Croatia bred, Ohio fed.**

—Stipe Miocic, UFC heavyweight champion

Photo courtesy of Koch family

We are African.
We are American.

—Mezi (age 7) and Mimi (age 9) Koch

Grampa refused to speak Italian.
"English!"

—Josie Cannella

The *y* makes a *j* sound.

—Rose G. (age 16)

**Slowly forgetting my language.
Sorry, Mom.**

—Loht P.

America changed
my phở too much.

—Nhung P. (age 15)

"You're Indian,
but have no accent?"

—Gaurav Ragtah

Grandparents found love during Korean War.

—Heather Rodstrom

SNUCK ACROSS THE BORDER . . . OF CANADA.

—Beth Van

Greek teen wanted away from WWI.

—Alicia Lundquist

Gypsy meets Lady Liberty at sixteen.

—Beja Marshall

Separated seven years, father a stranger.

—Jen Min Kuo

I Am Becoming an Immigrant Again

By Quynh Nguyen Trinh

Photo by Chanda Williams

I don't take my American citizenship for granted. That's why Thanksgiving is so important to my family. You know those Thanksgiving food drives where people donate turkey and canned goods for families in need? When we resettled here from Vietnam in the 1970s, we were one of those families. That's when we knew the generosity and character of this country.

My earliest memories involve food: At age six, wondering why a pork roll had been tossed aside as we escaped on one of the last helicopter flights to leave Vietnam; then trying my first Hershey bar and fruit cocktail from a can on a boat to Guam. At age seven, after settling in Minnesota, forming an assembly line in our kitchen and making bánh baos (steamed dumplings) to sell at the local grocery store to earn extra money. That was our first entrepreneurial endeavor in America.

In my forties, after many career successes, I asked myself, "What is my purpose, my legacy?" The answer tied my past to my future: bánh mì.

This humble Vietnamese sandwich honors my journey. Both of my parents were Vietnamese-French-Chinese, so the bánh mì signifies my heritage. It reflects the French influence in Vietnamese culture, the history of our war-torn country, and my pilgrimage to the US, the place where I found my voice.

Five years ago in Atlanta, if you wanted a bánh mì, you had to go to Buford Highway—our ethnic corridor—miles from my home in East Atlanta Village. We were still in a recession: who would spend $5 in gas for a $3 sandwich? Making bánh mì was something I could embrace that would allow me to give back to my community.

I started We Suki Suki in an eight-by-fifty-foot storefront, with two George Foreman grills and a toaster oven. I applied the principles you learn when you first emigrate. Those are humble beginnings: you don't have credit, you can't borrow; you have to be resourceful and make do.

Bánh mì has given me purpose. I wanted authenticity without losing integrity, so I began each morning the traditional way, selecting vegetables from the market like they do in Vietnam. I marinated my own meats, pickled my own veggies, and sourced the bread from local Vietnamese bakers. A bánh mì is the sum of its parts: everything is essential, nothing more, nothing less. If I'm going to make you wait for a sandwich, it has to be a sandwich worth waiting for.

Every chef goes through a journey with food, which often returns to whatever one's mom or grandmother cooked—food from the heart. What started as a one-woman operation has become a community partnership known as the Global Grub Collective, featuring twenty home cooks sharing their love for food from around the world. Together we're paying tribute to where we came from and sharing our heritage with our fellow Americans.

Quynh Trinh is a cyclical entrepreneur and brand builder who makes Atlanta her home with her two boys.

Land of opportunity,
if you're resourceful.

—James Glover

Left Spain for love.
Found home.

—Juan Alvarez

"What IS that in your lunchbox?"

—Lee-Sean Huang

Can't find Guilin rice noodles
anywhere.

—Linda Ge

NO FAMILIAR FACES
ON THE TV.

—Ryan Potter

I am not your "model minority."

–Davin Loh

Nah, dog. It's cool. I'm white.

–Himanshu Kumar Suri, aka "Heems"

MOM PROTECTED ME WITH AMERICAN NAME.

–Christopher Wedge

AFRICAN IMMIGRANTS, REFUGEES: DIASPORA'S OUR HOME.

–Lula Saleh

Memories still vivid. Accent slowly fading.

–Carlos Murawczyk

Salvadoran immigrant raises
US Navy diver.

—Chris Butler

THE SHIP'S NAME WAS CHARMING NANCY.

—Candy Cooper McDowall

Two on Mayflower, rest in steerage.

—T. McKinley

The passenger list preserves their names.

—Barbara Quintiliano

SEASICK 10 DAYS.
HAPPY 75 YEARS.

—Lisa Kothe

Photo courtesy of Rashid family

"I didn't speak for a year."

—Akil Rashid (bottom row, second from left), age 5,
upon moving from Tanzania to the United States

MY UNCLE SPONSORED MY ENTIRE FAMILY.

—Naciye Emren

From nothing we all became something.

—Bo Thao-Urabe

SOUTHEAST ASIA FELL, REFUGEE STORY BEGAN.

—Ka Vang

Moroccan made fearless by male-dominated society.

—Sanaa Hamri

Taiwanese and American: both, not either.

—Jaime Yen

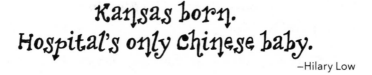

Kansas born.
Hospital's only Chinese baby.

—Hilary Low

Black Latina.
Slave ship stopped everywhere.

—Veronica Chambers

Grandma's serving platter
has survived generations.

—Alicia Salas

Bagels best with American free press.

—Sharon Hessney

Black beans and lechon asado:
Thanksgiving.

—Christina Gonzalez-Aguirre

Twenty Lost Years, Capped by Blessing

By Fbm Fidel Nshombo

In 1998, I was still a teen starting secondary school in Bukavu, Democratic Republic of the Congo. My father's photography business was growing while my mother was, well, the mother, making sure her eleven children were well cared for.

After the First Congo War that ousted dictator Mobutu Sese Seko in 1996, followed by a brief time of crimes and killings, the Second Congo War started in 1998. Gunshots could be heard from every corner of the city. Bad memories of the day that Mobutu's fighter jets dropped missiles in Bukavu would come to mind when clouds changed from blue to gray like it was getting ready to rain. But it was not about to rain; gray clouds were signs of evil happening in my city. Students were running frantically, attempting to escape capture as the military trucks drove through the school yard. I jumped the fence and ran with a couple of friends. I checked home, where I found no one, so we sought refuge in the church.

I never thought I would be homeless in my own country.

The priest at the church helped us move to Uvira, a small city one hundred kilometers away. To survive, the other kids and I started scavenging for food and begging on the street. I never thought I would be homeless in my own country. The UN Refugee Agency couldn't help us because we were internal refugees.

In 1999, Uvira was under siege. With my four friends, I crossed into Burundi, seeking refuge. We then canoed to Tanzania and Zambia, where we were separated after being spotted by police. I arrived in Zimbabwe after weeks of walking, canoeing, and hitchhiking without a passport.

In Zimbabwe I came to terms with the fact that I was an orphan, living on my own. I had to lie about my age in order to be left alone. In less than a year, I teamed up with a group of refugee activists to advocate against the mistreatment of refugees in Zimbabwe. This action unleashed a series of events that caused seventy-eight innocent refugees to be imprisoned and deported by the Zimbabwean government.

I was on the run to avoid deportation. After three years as a fugitive through Botswana, South Africa, Namibia, and Angola, I found myself in Zimbabwe again in 2004, where I was arrested on the activism charges and for speaking out against the injustice.

The UN Refugee Agency advocated for my release and promised to help get my documents back. But before that could happen, I was kidnapped, tortured, and deported to Mozambique by Zimbabwean secret agents. The Mozambique police deported me back to Zimbabwe, accusing me of being a trafficker. After weeks of being thrown from one jail to another, the UN Refugee Agency finally located me and advocated for my release again. This time they worked hard to secure me a visa to safety.

In June 2006, I was handed a plastic bag and told that I was going to the United States. When I opened the package, it read that I was headed to Boise, Idaho, a city that I'd never heard of, never dreamed of, but a place that today I call home. Ten years of wars, running, suffering, and escaping death were capped with a joyful and prosperous ending.

Today in Boise, I celebrate positive experiences every year. These include finding out that my family was still alive, getting married to the love of my life, having children of my own, and publishing books about my plight. Today my parents live in Canada while my wife, my five daughters, and I are in Boise. Boise is a place where I watch my children go to bed every night without hearing the sounds of gunshots, a place where I enjoy the peace and freedom that I was denied everywhere I lived before. People often ask me if I miss Congo, the culture, the people, and the food. I respond "no," because Congo has always resided in me.

Fidel Nshombo is the author of Route to Peace *and* Route to Peace 2. *He has been awarded the Refugee Integration and Success Award by the Idaho Office of Refugees, as well as recognized by Boise's mayor as an "Honored Boise Citizen."*

IMMIGRANT, WRITER, DAUGHTER, SISTER, MOTHER, SURVIVOR.

—Edwidge Danticat

Refugees: victims of terror, not terrorists.

—David Miliband, president and CEO, International Rescue Committee

BOOM! CRACK! POW! IT'S QUIET NOW.

—Cairo Grace

Five tickets to freedom in paradise.

—Roberto Soto

"Is your name on the list?"

—Ibochawa Kabwaii

IN USA, DIAL 2 FOR SPANISH!

—Alex Gerson

Got on wrong train. Became Iowans.

—Seth Boffeli

My Father Survived. Now I Must.

By Lisa Klug

My father was born to a Jewish family in Poland in 1923. During his childhood, his family moved from a little shtetl, or village, to the independent city-state of Danzig, a metropolis bordered by Germany and Poland. German culture heavily influenced Danzig (now Gdańsk), and with the rise of National Socialism, my father was only a boy when the anti-Jewish Nuremberg Laws ultimately expelled him from school.

He also witnessed Kristallnacht, the massive pogrom known as the "Night of Broken Glass," when Nazis attacked Jews and their homes and shops. When World War II broke out in 1939, my father was sixteen. He was one of five immediate family members and hundreds of other relatives trapped in Europe. Although they escaped to Poland, within days the Nazis invaded and forced them into a ghetto and slave labor. My father's eldest brother had miraculously escaped to Panama, and later, the US, where after six long years, he obtained a visa for my father, whom American troops liberated from Buchenwald in 1945. He weighed only sixty pounds, was near death with typhus, and had been traumatized by the torture he'd endured. Even though he often asked why he survived and not his loved ones, he was determined to live, and after two years, he could walk again.

With his Old World Yiddish expressions and love of Jewish tradition, my father was part dad and part granddad, and he encouraged me to "make the most of life," especially during our most challenging moments. Because he had witnessed the worst in humanity, nothing made him happier than seeing people express loving kindness toward one another. I became obsessed with my father's story. I interviewed him endlessly, researched his persecution records, fought and won a ghetto pension claim, and videotaped our roots trip to Europe, where he recited the mourner's prayer for his family and friends and tested his DNA to perhaps find lost relatives—without success.

Even when dementia plagued him, he never forgot the war, which pained me so much. When he died a few years ago, at age ninety-one, I buried him in Jerusalem and included the names of his family on his tombstone so they could finally have a memorial of their own. My father's survival is a source of great resilience and inspiration. As his survivor, I have a responsibility to honor his legacy, and share his gratitude for the shelter the US can provide those most in need.

Lisa Klug, the author of Cool Jew *and* Hot Mamalah*, has written for the* New York Times, The Times of Israel, *and* Variety.

90

A BETTER LIFE FOR OUR CHILDREN.

—Mila Kunis

*Separated by war,
family is forever.*

—Steven Huan Thai

1976. Sought American dream
as cashier.

—Tanvi Rastogi, about her mother who immigrated
to the United States from India

Escape Cossacks;
one suitcase; Shabbos candlesticks.

—Myra Paull

Canadian's "eh's" got teased outta me.

—Gillian Zoe Segal

Refugee went from burkas
to bachelors.

—Hangama Asefi

Sister pretends she can't use chopsticks.

—Yukari Iwatani Kane

As American as . . . tacos al pastor.

—Fred Vega

I only speak Spanish on weekends.

—Ally Bravo (age 14)

"No good grades, no food tonight."

—Gerrie Lim

The force behind my dragon mom.

—Cathleen Chin

Photo courtesy of NASA

From migrant farmworker to NASA astronaut.

—José M. Hernández, mission specialist STS-128 *Discovery*

Farmers in Norway.
Farmers in Midwest.

—John Evenson

**Aimed for education;
became an educator.**

—David Da Wei Liu

**Grandson of immigrants,
now immigrants' advocate.**

—Jeffrey Baron

**Building the America
of Dad's dreams.**

—David Henry Hwang

Retired Marine, looked upon as outsider.

—Steven Maravillas

Delinquencia.
Enfermedad.
Pobreza.
Arriesgado.
Oportunidades.
Friendship.

—Jennifer M. A.

تركت من أحب لأجل من أحب.

[Translation:]

Left my loves for my love.

—Shorq Alqahimi

polyglot, cooked with the world. joyous.

–Mario Batali

One side Pilgrims.
Other fled Communists.

—Alex Lin-Moore

CZECHOSLOVAKIA.
THE UNBEARABLE
LIGHTNESS OF FLEEING.

—Theresa Ralston

Fled Nasser's Alexandria; drafted upon arrival.

—Charles Braunstein

My mom still yells on FaceTime.

—Seivi Katro

IMMIGRANT PARENTS GRANTED
AMNESTY BY REAGAN.

—Edwin Coronel

A Young Refugee's Journey Through Emoji

By Huong T. Nguyen, Vietnam

Illustration by Lila Volkas

When I left my country at age five, I did not have words to understand my refugee experience. I chose emojis to tell my story as they more accurately represent my understanding of the experience at that time.

I was a **baby chick**, just two years old, when Saigon fell in 1975. My father was in the Southern Vietnamese army and served as a translator for the American forces during the American War (as Vietnamese referred to it). The victors forced my father into a "reeducation" camp. When released, he promptly bought a fishing boat, loaded my two older sisters and others onto it, and set sail for international waters, hoping to escape Communist oppression. A French vessel picked up his boat, and he and my sisters were eventually settled in the United States. My mother, my younger brother, and I tried to escape together two times, only to be captured and sent back to Vietnam. Lack of money forced my mother to send me alone with my two aunts and my cousin on my last journey. I was five years old and apparently worth two thin bars of gold.

The **waves** carried my two aunts, my cousin, and me to Malaysia. My mother brought me to the docks and handed me to her oldest sister. We were packed onto an overcrowded, dilapidated fishing boat and set sail for international waters. Some boats floated to their destinations; others sank. To me, the black water was awesome and scary at the same time. I still feel the same way about the waves today, nearly forty years later.

I was five years old and apparently worth two thin bars of gold.

The **skull and crossbones** represent pirates. People escaping Vietnam by boat were known to bring their valuable possessions with them. This attracted pirates from Vietnam and surrounding countries. Sometimes pirates would rob these refugees of their jewelry, other times their dignity, and others their lives.

When pirates from Thailand boarded our boat, my aunt placed her **diamond ring** in my mouth. I sat with this ring in my mouth, trying to make myself invisible, as the pirates broke my other aunt's jade bracelets and stole them. Luckily, those pirates stole only jewelry on our boat. My aunt's quick thinking allowed us to sell the ring at a refugee camp to buy a month's worth of food.

The **tent** reminds me of the two refugee camps that took us in. From the second one in Malaysia we sent word to my dad who, along with the Catholic church in Green Bay, Wisconsin, sponsored our trip to the United States.

The **airplane** (actually, several) carried us from Kuala Lumpur to Hong Kong to Chicago, and then to Green Bay. We arrived in the dead of winter. When I saw my father again, he wrapped me in a large faux leopard-skin coat. At the airport, many people came to welcome us to our new country.

Huong T. Nguyen is an attorney living in the San Francisco Bay Area with her wife and two sons.

My parents met in ESL class.

—Lalo Alcarez

Irreverent descendant of
religious freedom seekers.

—Jacqueline Rice

13: LEFT SWITZERLAND.
93: STILL YODELING.

—Kitty Maguire

Came by force, stayed by choice.

—Micaela Davis

Learned English
in under six months.

—Roberta Brodsky Connors

HOLOCAust survivor:
i inherit GRANdFAther's CANteen.

—Cindy Tebo

Half Jewish, half Armenian: all survivor.

—Amy Keyishian

Wanted to give Mom my birthright.

—Shauna Greene

IRISH TEENAGER FOUND REFUGE AT YWCA.

—Heather McFarland-Ribbs

Antique Eenglish rings on American fingers.

—Susan Lake

ALBANIAN OLYMPIAN FLEES FOR AMERICA: REBORN.

—Enkelejda Shehaj

I Stayed and I Raised Myself

By Ikram Goldman

I was born and raised in Israel by Christian Arab parents. I went to private schools, and English was my third language. Being able to speak English meant access and superiority in a country that suppressed Arabs.

When I was thirteen, my mother fell ill suddenly and needed cancer treatment, which only a hospital in Chicago was able to provide at the time. (Subsequently, a hospital in Israel became the number one treatment center in the world for exactly the cancer that brought my mother to America.) My mother, as sick as she was, did not want to leave my brother and me behind. It was partly because we were young, but also, I later realized, because we spoke English and she didn't.

We flew KLM from Israel to the United States, and the seats were huge! At least that was what I remembered from that time, until I flew back to Israel twenty-five years later with my twin boys, and the seats were miniscule. I remember wondering how my mother did it with two kids in tow.

When we first landed in New York to be transferred to Chicago, I was blown away by everyone at the airport. It was full of people from every part of the world, but the one thing I remember they all had in common was that they all spoke English. I remember turning to my mom and saying to her in Arabic: "Mom, *everyone* here speaks English!"

The plan was to go back to Israel. But my mom passed away shortly after we arrived, and I realized I didn't want to leave. I stayed and I raised myself.

Ikram Goldman owns ikram, a women's clothing store in Chicago. She is known, among other things, for dressing former first lady Michelle Obama.

Photo by Josh Goldman

Glimpsed at citizenship test;
I'd fail!

—Jayden Gino Price

Gained: American passport.
Lost: mother tongue.

—Grace Prasad

**Zeal to assimilate
killed a language.**

—H. M. Stiller

**Canadian, except not
polite or friendly.**

—Linwood Boomer

THIRD CULTURE KID,
FOUND NEW HOME.

—Gari De Ramos

Indian mother:
Ford's first female engineer.

—Dr. Sanjay Gupta

Constant restlessness, in search of *home*.

—Toyin Ojih Odutola

No money.
No English.
Just grit.

—Andrea Brinn

Grandfather, eight,
came alone on ship.

—Lydia Hall

Just the clothes on his back.

—Marisela Bravo-Parker

"So Many Things to Tell You"

By Diane Guerrero

Photo courtesy of Diane Guerrero

For a long time, I would cringe every time my mother would call me. There was even an eight-year period when I didn't talk to her or see her. My family is from Colombia, and most of them are still there. Occasionally they send me pictures, stories, letters—little reminders of my family history to let me know that there are people in Colombia who love me. Sometimes I see these and I'm touched; other times I just let it go. I think it's because I'm so overwhelmed every day by images and information that sometimes paying attention to my own life can be hard.

Recently, a relative sent me a picture, a single image that changed the way I feel about my family. Usually when I see something that reminds me of my childhood, it's difficult for me. But this photo made me really happy. So I sent it to my mother. I figured it would make her smile. In truth, I didn't want it to evoke too much of a dialogue; we rarely talked.

Then something happened that doesn't usually happen: my mother called me and I answered. She started telling me about that day in the picture. She told me that photo was taken on a hot summer day in Passaic, New Jersey, when I was about three. That morning, she'd had a specific vision for an outfit for me. She said she always woke up like that: thinking about how to dress me up, how to style my hair, relishing compliments from strangers about her darling daughter. This outfit was a polka-dot bathing suit, paired with striped shorts and polka-dot sunglasses—she felt it was "so fashion forward." She said she had all these hopes and dreams for me. She saw that I was always performing and wanted to be in front of people and make people laugh. "Oh, I wanted to take you on all these auditions," she said, "but your father would shoot me down and say, 'No, you're not taking my daughter anywhere; it's dangerous.'"

She wanted to expose me to the world of acting and fashion and so much more. I've always had this notion that if I had started in show business earlier, my family life would have been different. If I had been working as a little girl and able to help take care of the family financially, we would have been fine.

My parents had been deported. I was left behind.

Then Mom said her new dream was for us to take a trip together and sit under a palm tree and just talk. "Diane, I have so many things to tell you," she said. And then I asked my mom something I never had considered before: "Mom, what were your hopes and dreams?" She just repeated, "So many things to tell you."

Mom had so many things to tell me because I really didn't know who she was. At the age of sixteen and living with my family in Boston, I returned home from school one day and walked into an empty house. I couldn't find my parents anywhere. Then I found out that they had been taken by immigration officers and deported to Colombia. I was left behind.

Every phone call after that from my parents was hard, but especially from my mom. I felt that she had failed me in some way. When I would talk to her, I would be angry. *This isn't fair. Why is this happening to me? I hate you. I don't know who you are.* So I stopped talking to her.

But this day was different. I was letting her in, and I was talking to her. Her words were so tender and patient and beautiful and poetic. All these memories of us together started flashing before my eyes. I felt her touch. I felt her kiss. I could smell her. And I thought: *Oh Mama, I've missed you. I need you.* I had forgotten about all that. I forgot my mother was there until someone removed her from me against her will. And then I realized something so second nature to most, but a new feeling for me: my mother loves me.

Diane Guerrero is an American actress known for her roles as Maritza Ramos on Orange Is the New Black *and Lina on* Jane the Virgin. *She is the author of a memoir,* In the Country We Love: My Family Divided.

NO REST WHILE FAMILIES REMAIN APART.

—Amanda Plummer

They called me "gringo" in Colombia.

—Daniel Renjifo

Immigrant parents, citizen children: successful together.

—Juan Ramirez

I wish they taught me Tagalog.

—Kristenelle Coronado

Imported by Quakers to fight Indians.

—Elizabeth Fleming

Fleeing Cold into Loneliness's Sharp Corner

By Osama Alomar

Translation by C. J. Collins

In 2008, when I told my friends that I wanted to immigrate to America, their reactions were mixed. Some of them opposed the idea, insisting that my situation in Syria was fine and might be improved if I put in more effort. They said there was nothing in the world like one's homeland, even if it had some negative aspects. Other friends showed a kind of jealousy mixed with flattery, and invitations to lunch or dinner adorned with excessive expressions of love and appreciation started to appear. For the first time in my life I felt like they were strangers to me, these friends from my student years who had been my companions in travel and parties, with whom I had wandered the streets and chased after girls. They had suddenly become far away from me. Isn't flattery a kind of exile? Often someone's mere expression of a desire for success can be the cause of our exclusion and imprisonment in the sharp corner of loneliness.

I don't know why I felt a longing for my homeland even before I had left it. Maybe it was a hidden feeling that some disaster would strike? But the idea of immigration to America had long before taken over my life. I needed to accomplish my only goal: to establish my name as a writer and a poet.

Searching for new horizons
In my little room in the Damascus suburbs.
A rain of farewell calls pours down on me,
A flood of feelings wearing me out.
Scents of failed loves stories waft from my pores.
In vain I try to escape them.
In vain I try to wash my soul.
Threads of tangled feelings pull me in all directions,
White threads . . . and gray ones.
Black threads . . .
And others that spin in my depths,
A whirlwind of a thousand rainbows.

When the airplane took off from Damascus International Airport and turned in its wide circle, I felt my life turning with it, full of the soul's fuel that is never spent.

Upon my arrival in the US, my cousin welcomed me at O'Hare Airport in Chicago, his face marked with fatigue from continuous work. When I had been here two months, he said to me, "I think you have no choice other than to work as a taxi driver." I felt like

"Did you immigrate to America to become a taxi driver?"

a giant hand had, with one blow, kidnapped my soul and all its dreams and hopes. Countless voices inside my head asked me, "Did you immigrate to America to become a taxi driver?" Some of them I recognized very well, others I could not. Some were polluted with gloating, and some adorned with love.

Four days later I was driving a yellow taxicab full of passengers, the sweat pouring off me. Since that day I have been searching for my lost soul, like a ship adrift in the midst of storms searches for a sheltering island where it can catch its breath.

Osama Alomar is the author of Fullblood Arabian, *which has been translated into English. His newest book is* The Teeth of the Comb and Other Stories, *published by New Directions.*

I am an Indian . . . from India.

—Annu Palakunnathu Matthew

*If not Native,
you're an immigrant.*

—Sarah Jones

**Hmong. China, Laos,
now America. Home.**

—Cualeng Vang

Quakers plus crackers:
New World mutt.

—Tom Price

**EASIER TO SAY THAN
IT LOOKS.**

—Cherry Chevapravatdumrong

First question: "Where's Michael Jordan's house?"

—Ivan Silva

MY STOWAWAY FOREFATHER WASN'T DEPORTED . . . WHEW!

—Ron Howard

Learned Vietnamese mom's recipes via YouTube.

—Jennifer N.

Teacher made me friend the FOB.

—Gene Leun Yang

Identity reduced to a checked box.

—A. McClure

Sesame Street's Olivia teaches me English.

—Diana Burbano

Obaachan Could Not Lock Past Away

By Teresa Tauchi

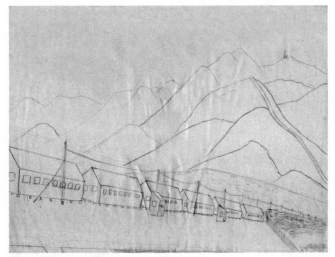

Illustration by Kiyono Tauchi

In 1944, my grandmother drew this illustration, a forty-five-year-old woman's perspective on the harsh, desolate setting that would be her home for the two and a half years after she and my grandfather were involuntarily relocated to the internment camp at Gila River, Arizona. Their five-year-old son, Shigeto, an only child, never made it; he had fallen ill while living at the pre-camp assembly center at Santa Anita, a converted racetrack, and died at L.A. County Hospital two years earlier.

How does one recover from the death of a child? My grandparents had struggled with infertility well into the second decade of their marriage and didn't become parents until their late thirties. If the birth of their son created a new family equilibrium, then his passing nearly destroyed it. Still, they wanted a legal heir. When the war was over, they offered to adopt their grown nephew. And so it was that in February 1950, my twenty-year-old dad sailed from Japan to join his new parents. Primogeniture has always been at the core of the Japanese family institution, and my dad's uncle—now his father—had done the same thing some thirty-five years prior, crossing the Pacific to become the adopted son of his uncle and to carry on the Tauchi family name.

Photo courtesy of Tauchi family

My grandparents created a new life for my dad, and in return he created a new family for them. My dad became fluent in English, received two degrees from UCLA, and served as an IBM company man for several decades. He was also able to bring a Japanese wife to the US, purchase a large ranch-style home in the Northern California suburbs, and support three generations living in one household.

My grandfather was a reticent man who rarely spoke of his family's suffering at the hands of the US government. Yet he did once tell me of the Caucasian friends who were brave and kind during the war and promised to harbor the few precious belongings he couldn't bear to destroy—the so-called "evidence" of his loyalty to the emperor of Japan.

My grandmother did not—or could not—keep the past locked away. The loss of her son remained at the center of her being. She kept framed photos of him in her bedroom and recounted his stories constantly. When I was a child, I thought that my brother looked a lot like my deceased uncle—they shared the same moon face and banged haircut. My mother later recalled that after my brother was born, my grandmother would spend hours alone with him in a secluded part of the house (he was her favorite grandchild, of course). And in the final days of my grandmother's life, just two weeks shy of her ninety-ninth birthday, when her physical demise would rob her of her ability to eat, walk, or communicate, she would from time to time cry out "Shigeto, Shigeto," or just quietly weep.

Teresa Tauchi is a marketing consultant who lives with her family in Oakland, California.

Even after internment, still love America.

—George Takei

Girl on plane to Miami, alone.

—Ileana Oroza

**An African seed
growing within America.**

—Rocky Dawuni

*An unlikely socialite:
this first-generation American.*

—Betty Wallace

Pregnant on boat.
Hid Jewish identity.

—Megan Mustoe

Even water tasted sweeter
in America.

—Joseph Hui

GRANDMOTHER DIDN'T TAKE HER
ERWTENSOEP LIGHTLY.

—Susan Breeden

Cheeseburga (cheeseburga)
deluxe: perfect Greek souvlaki.

—Panayota Liopyris

She has two birthdays we celebrate.

—Alexandra Mantas

Me:
smorgasbord of Portuguese, Chinese, Hawaiian.

—Nol Martín-Tungpalan

Filipino-American.
I'm the hyphen in between.

—Deidrene Crisanto

PICTURE MENU AT MCDONALD'S, FIRST HAMBURGER.

—Chanel Kim

Learned English from Doctor Seuss books.

—Crista Johnson

Eight hours English, five hours Spanish.

—Frida Flores

FAMILY VACATION: TWENTY-FIVE HOURS TO ASIA.

—Jay Naka (age 6)

PAID FAMILY'S DEBTS VIA AMERICAN DREAM.

—Robbie Tseng

Always Called a White Guy "Sir"

By Victor Elán Vazquez

Photo courtesy of Victor Elán Vazquez

Mom and Dad have become United States citizens. They've been married for thirty years. The effort was a long time coming. They were both afraid of what a new administration might do. On a cold day in December 2016, Obama welcomed 2,301 individuals, via video, to this country immediately after they made an oath.

Mom (Angelica) was eleven when she came from Mexico; Dad (also Victor) was sixteen. They are now fifty-one and sixty, respectively.

DAD: I picked almonds and grapes before I became a DJ. I played Michael Jackson a lot. Everyone always went crazy for Michael.

MOM: That's why our firstborn is named Michael.

DAD: She sold clothes back then.

MOM: We met when he came into my store, looking for jeans. Someone else was assisting him. He didn't know how to ask for the right size. He hadn't learned how to say the number twenty-eight. I stepped in and helped.

DAD: I didn't know how to count. You tell me if you know how to count in a different language. It's hard! If I wanted two cheeseburgers, one for me and one for your mother, I used to order them at the counter by pointing and saying, "One cheeseburger and one cheeseburger." I didn't know how to say two.

MOM: You did know how to be polite.

DAD: I always called a white guy "sir." The first lesson I learned out on the field: never run. Keep your dignity. I would stand up and look at the deportation officers in the eyes. I needed them to see me.

MOM: We learned a lot of things together, and our world is a lot different now. We have homes across California.

DAD: I'm a real estate broker with my own office. I drive clients around Los Angeles in my new Prius. I call it my little *huevito*.

MOM: Which means egg.

DAD: Each time I sell a house I take a photo of the people and their new home. I buy them a bottle of something. We celebrate. I help people find their dream homes.

MOM: The American dream: taking root, finding home.

DAD: When Mexico sends its people, it sends the best because it's people like us who are fighters for peace, love, humility, grace, justice, and joy. We are here, and we are fathers, mothers, sisters, brothers, neighbors, friends.

MOM: The stranger at the store not knowing how to ask for something in a new language.

DAD: Just you wait; that stranger might help you or your kids find their perfect home one day.

Victor Elán Vazquez is a writer, playwright, and son of immigrant parents. He is a PEN Center USA Emerging Voices fellow and a Lambda Literary Emerging LGBT writer.

"Hello, sir, do you remember me?"*

—Paul Sonenberg

*"That's what clients always say to me when they call on the phone," says Sonenberg, a supervising attorney at Community Refugee and Immigration Services in Columbus, Ohio.

From Spain to Hawaii, chopping sugarcane.

—Bethany Nickless Meyer

AFRICAN-AMERICAN + FRENCH + SCOTTISH. STIRRED, NOT SHAKEN.

—China Forbes

MY FAMILY'S FROM TAIWAN, NOT CHINA.

—Andrew Chen

Look! Dad brought the wok camping.

—Amy Wang

Half American, half Mexican, all soccer.

—Omar V. (age 11)

GREAT-GREAT-GRANDFATHER PETER IMMIGRATED; I'M A PETERSON.

—Allen Peterson

Border guard wouldn't spell family name.

—Richard M. Johnson

The other kids never had grebble.

—Michelle Wolff

GRANDMA USED ONE ENGLISH WORD: LAZY.

—Ben Roberts

Bruce Lee, my only movie hero.

—Phil Yu, aka "Angry Asian Man"

India the mother, America the provider.

—Naeem Khan

Eighties Detroit radio,
my America lens.

—Vikki Tobak

MIX OF CALYPSO, BOLLYWOOD,
AND ROCK-AND-ROLL.

—Neesha Hosein

Five generations
from immigrant to artist.

—Lori Sulzberger

Their old neighborhood is
"fashionable" today.

—Jonathan Zipper

I Am an American Without Papers

By Jose Antonio Vargas

Photo by Gerry Salva-Cruz

My grandfather immigrated legally to the United States in 1984. He worked as a security guard, saving up money to bring me to America and get me a green card. I arrived when I was twelve and enjoyed a "normal" life here. When I was sixteen, I went to the DMV to get my driver's permit and learned that the green card he'd procured for me was fake. I was a boy who had lived in and loved America; now I learned that I was an "illegal alien." For the first time I felt that I didn't belong here.

Soon after, I discovered my calling. My high school English teacher said I was asking too many annoying questions and that I should explore this thing I didn't know much about called "journalism." So I went to a journalism summer camp. At first it was weird to see my name on the byline on a piece of paper. Then I thought: *If I don't have the right papers to be in America, then at least my name will be on the paper.* I decided I could just write my way into America. Over the next fourteen years, I wrote for the *San Francisco Chronicle* and worked on staff at the *Washington Post.* I wrote about important political events, profiled big names, and covered groundbreaking stories—all while hiding that I wasn't really supposed to be here.

Then I landed the biggest writing assignment of my life: a profile of Mark Zuckerberg for *The New Yorker.* During one of five interviews with Mark, he turned to me and said, "Jose, where are you from?"

Where are you from? At that point in my life I couldn't honestly answer that question. At a time when I thought I had succeeded in America—by way of professional success, paying taxes, and contributing to a country I called home—I still couldn't go to Mexico for a friend's wedding or visit my family. I hadn't seen my mom in nineteen years, but knew if I went to the Philippines I wouldn't be able to come back.

That's when I realized I'd had enough. After fourteen years in hiding, I decided to come forward and do so in the most public way possible. I wrote an essay called "My Life as an Undocumented Immigrant" for the *New York Times*. This was the first time I had written about immigration. I had spent nearly a decade and a half ignoring it.

Immigration remains the most controversial yet least understood issue in America. People simply do not know how it works and ask me the same kinds of questions, no matter where I'm speaking. As a result, I've become a walking uncomfortable conversation. I'm asked if I'm Mexican. I'm not, I'm from the Philippines, and my Spanish name is because Spain went to the Philippines in 1521 and stayed for three hundred years. Contrary to what many people believe, not everyone undocumented is Mexican; in fact, one million of the eleven million undocumented people in the country are actually from Asia and the Pacific Islands, like me.

People ask why I haven't been deported. I do not know. The Obama administration deported more than two million immigrants—a record.

Exactly how many millions the Trump administration will deport is unknown. But what we do know is the Trump administration's executive orders on immigration have caused unprecedented panic and palpable fear among immigrants and our families. As a presidential candidate, Donald Trump ran the most anti-immigrant campaign in modern American history. So far, as president, Trump is delivering on the promise to purge America of its immigrants, documented and undocumented.

People ask why I chose to come out about my legal status, and why others are choosing to do so. I say: we're not really coming out, we're just letting you in.

Jose Antonio Vargas is a Pulitzer Prize–winning journalist, filmmaker, and entrepreneur. He is the founder and CEO of Define American, a nonprofit media and culture organization that seeks to elevate the conversation about immigration and citizenship in America, and the founder of #EmergingUS, a media startup that lives at the intersection of race, immigration, and identity in a multicultural America and is the first-ever media property owned by an undocumented immigrant.

Ancestors: 1632.
Daughter: 1993.
All undocumented.

—Chris Hoeckley

Brush Your Teeth. Because You Can.

By Angelica Lai

Even when I was seven, I was jealous of my classmates when they would complain about going to the dentist. Insurance was a luxury. Dentists were luxuries. Choices were luxuries. But a smile was important, and I knew that. So I brushed and gargled and pretended I had dentist stories when my friends talked about their dentist visits.

My dad never really knew how to smile. Photographs of him always showed the same hard-pressed lips, but he loved being behind the camera. A lot of his money would go into developing photos and the fifty-plus albums stacked in our closets. He captured our young faces, we who could laugh anytime we wanted to in front of anyone, who could eat anything we wanted anywhere, who didn't need to learn how to smile.

My dad, a Vietnamese refugee, prided himself on his will. He had gone to other countries—Guam and parts of Asia—with little money in his pockets. He could persuade his peers to think one way one day, and the next way the next. He donated money when he had none to spare.

But he could not eat meat or broccoli or other hard things. When you're escaping a war and trying to keep your parents and eight younger siblings safe, you don't think about teeth. When you're trying to feed everyone crammed in a small house in Guam, you don't think about teeth. My dad didn't think about teeth. Not until he had children.

Every time we went out to eat, we would always order a dish that had tofu in it. My dad hated tofu, but it was soft. He would try to eat the beef or the chicken, but when we left the restaurant, there would always be a pile of chewed meat covered with a napkin on his plate.

Whenever I came home for breaks from school, my dad would make me take him out for lunch every day. These lunches would usually be spent in silence or with him making a few observations about people in the restaurant. *Those two have probably been friends for a long time*, he would say, or *the waiter forgot to give that lady her water*.

A little over a month before he was hospitalized for a heart attack, he asked me to take him out for lunch again. We were sitting in a Cantonese restaurant. He said he wanted to sit us all down and talk to us. *There is still a lot to say*, he said.

That day at the Cantonese restaurant, he ordered duck noodle soup for me. It was his favorite as a kid, he said. I spent the entire meal staring at the tofu on his plate.

Angelica Lai is a writer from Guam whose published stories include "After Life" in the Columbia Journal *and "Two Tigers" in* Paper Darts.

Stolen birth certificate;
150 years American.

—D. B. Sherman

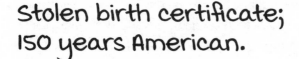

Puerto Rico, Manhattan:
both are islands.

—Ocean Jensen

Hoping my school lunch
doesn't "smell."

—Nikita Patel

Dad's story starts with slave ships. . . .*

—Christina Fields

*Mom's with escaping central Italian poverty.

Nana brought secrets:
the perfect marinara.

—Amanda Marini

ETHIOPIA
MY IDENTITY,
GURSHA
MY LIVELIHOOD.

—Getahun Asfaw

AMERICA GONNA
PANDA EXPRESS
CHIPOTLE
EVERYONE.

—Eddie Huang

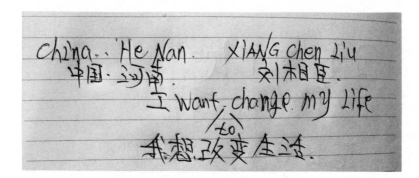

I want to change my life.

—Xiang Chen Liu

Note pinned to coat: Pittsburgh, USA.

—Sandi Woodward

WALKED FROM QUÉBEC TO NEW YORK.

—Peggy Freudenthal

Fled two continents. Met in Catskills.

—Sara Solnick

Yes, Sicilians are different from Italians.

—Rachel Driskell

GRANDMA'S SUNDAY GREETING: *GOTENYU ZISA BOYCHIKEL!**

—Steven Melnick

*Dear God, what a sweet boy!

Humiliation, Patience, Perseverance:
Path to Citizenship

By Najib Azhar

In the summer of 2000, a software company in California sponsored me, and I brought my family to the United States. In December 2002, I attended my nephew's wedding in Pakistan, my country of birth. During the brief time I was there, Pakistan was added to the flagged list of countries under the National Security Entry-Exit Registra- tion System (NSEERS). When I returned to California, I had to go through a secondary security screening before I was allowed to leave the airport. I waited in an empty room for several hours. Finally, an immigration offi- cer entered to ask me a series of questions: "Why were you in Pakistan? Are you affiliated with any groups in Pakistan? Who was in attendance at this wedding?" I answered all his questions and assumed the grueling process was finally over and that I could return home. Then he demanded that I report to the USCIS (United States Citizenship and Immigration Services) office in San Jose every few months. If I failed to comply, I would be considered out-of-status and deportable.

Profiling was an inescapable aspect of my family's life as immigrants.

And so I did, meticulously preparing all my documents and history, organizing them in color-coded folders, and tagging documents for easy retrieval. I over-prepared because I didn't know what to expect. The scene I was met with each time remains imprinted in my memory: over a hundred people, all men, of all ages, all looking deeply worried and confused. When my turn came, I was asked the same accusatory questions I'd heard at the airport regarding where I went and why. I was told to report back every few months at the office.

I have no doubt that the eight extra years that it took to get my family's green card was a domino effect of the NSEERS. For eight long years I checked the mail every day, anxious for progress, hoping we'd be able to move forward from this state of limbo. This discriminatory profiling was an inescapable aspect of my family's life as immigrants, an insurmountable obstacle to the better life we sought. The uncertainty we endured as our case remained in abeyance left us unsettled and hesitant to make a permanent home, fearing that our applications would be denied and that we would be deported.

Our financial instability was inevitable, as employers were unwilling to risk hiring me with my pending immigration status, despite my doctorate in bioengineering from Drexel University and master's degree in chemical engineering from Penn State. When my mother-in-law's Parkinson's disease took a turn for the worse, I hid the details of her sickness from my wife to reduce her mental anguish. We couldn't risk visiting her in Pakistan for fear of being denied reentry to the United States.

We refused to give up. We were one of the lucky families. If it were not for the financial help from family and friends, we would not have been able to hire an immigration attorney. Our attorney persistently questioned the legality of the government's policies, and we eventually earned our legal permanent residency in 2009. In 2014, we were naturalized as citizens, and we were elated to vote in our first election in 2016. And now—almost two decades after moving to this country— we fear are we, as a nation, back to square one?

Najib Azhar is a biomedical engineer specializing in medical instrumentation who lives with his wife in the San Francisco Bay Area.

2016: naturalized citizens watched America denature.

—Amit Majmudar

All colors become green on cards.

—Hebe Gutierrez

Photo by Adam Elkins

Photo by Adam Elkins

Ellis Island.
Don't have papers.
Smith?

—Ryann Smith

"Go back
to Africa."
Just might.

—Retha Simone

Photo by Adam Elkins

The Great war
extended Grandma's
vacation.

—Meg Edwards

Photo by Adam Elkins

Ramen noodles.
Vienna sausage.
The struggle.

—Yasmeen Harrison

Fried plantains in the Smoky Mountains

By Melanie Márquez Adams

Alone in my car, surrounded by tiny blue mountains, country and Christian music are the only options on the radio. I turn up the volume and wonder how much time is left before I get to my destination. Maybe I am already in southwest Virginia, or perhaps I haven't left Tennessee yet. Here, the borders are blurred and can get confusing. Suddenly, the background music turns into undulating notes full of memories taking me back to another time. A time of daily commuting to an office job in a Latin American metropolis, drowning in a sea of buildings, traffic, and countless billboard ads. I need a change of pace and choose a remote southern city in the big country to the north.

The harsh winter weather receives me when I set foot on this land for the first time. It seems like an affront to the suffocating heat that I leave behind in my coastal hometown in Ecuador. During the flight, I worry about not agreeing on a meeting point with the university worker. What if I miss my ride in a place where I don't know a soul? This concern vanishes, however, giving way to a worse one when I get a peek of the tiny airport, swallowed by the abundant snow. What have I done?

In the midst of the fog, the buildings are dissolved into mountains, the traffic into solitude, and the ads on the billboards into stern bible verses. The music of Appalachia becomes my new companion in the dance across my memories. The banjo twangs and I find myself at my first county fair, overwhelmed by the saturated smell of fried foods and the curious glance of a little blonde girl who finds me quite exotic. The fiddle vibrates with a high-pitched sound just like the southern accent with which my ears still struggle. The strings of the mandolin scratch the melody and I find myself in the middle of a classroom as the only Latin American student. The professor wants me to compare the topic at hand to the way things are in that picturesque place where he thinks I come from. I brew a colorful story, leaving the middle-aged academic satisfied with the ethnic minute of his class.

The banjo growls and resonates with mountains and more mountains, pasture and more pasture, railroads and more railroads, churches and more churches. Sometimes I feel paralyzed by the silence of rural life. But after the excitement of the big city wears off, in the midst of the incessant shriek of traffic, the constant crowd, and the landscape of buildings tightened against each other impeding the circulation of fresh air, I hear the mountains calling me. They whisper, to the rhythm of the wind, stories about the mines, the moonshine, the quilts, and the innocent happiness of their people.

Melanie Márquez Adams is a writer living in Tennessee.

Old sod to New
World tale.

—Jane Lynch

Twins assigned
different birthdates
upon arrival.

—Jordana Schmier

They traded skullcaps for baseball caps.

—Toby Manewith

Schnitzel princess brought
to burger country.

—Helena Pepper Bluhm

Grandfather taught me power of organizing.

–Julie Chávez Rodríguez, granddaughter of César Chávez

Joined the vast Midwestern Yugoslavian diaspora.

—Aleksandra Walker

Hessians who fought Americans, became them.

—Matthew Saunders

Tudors kept executing; seemed safer here.

—Cass Morris

My Arabic name doesn't mean terrorist.

—Anwar Mohammed (age 16)

"Dirty Guineas" turned into white folks.

—Renee Segreto

African blood
but also American spirit.

—Zakaria Modi

Arrived with suitcases and family recipes.

—Oksana Mykytyn

Crossed the Pacific,
seven months pregnant.

—Vilma Sanoy Pineda

Escaped invading army.
Served America instead.

—Jill Dunn

Couldn't spell Malamed;
meet the Millers.

—Quin Miller

Our America: Free, Brave, and Mashed-Up

Rebecca Lehrer and Amy S. Choi are friends, business partners, and the cofounders of The Mash-Up Americans, a publisher and creative studio that explores race, culture, identity, and what makes us who we are in America.

Photo by Duane Fernandez

REBECCA: I exist only because America, the land of immigrants and refugees, exists. My dad was born in Los Angeles to two immigrant parents—one from Poland and the other from Vienna. My grandmother came to the United States as a teenager, knowing just one distant aunt. Imagine! My mom emigrated from El Salvador. *Her* parents had emigrated from Germany to Latin America after being immigrants many times over throughout Europe. My grandfather eventually became the ambassador from El Salvador to Israel. My family's story deeply informs my understanding of community, identity, and family. There's blood family, and there's Diaspora family. I mean, if you are a Salvadoran Jew then we are forever deeply connected. And if you are an immigrant, we are part of another kind of family, the fabric that makes up what is beautiful about the United States. My six words on my family's story: "Spanglish is my best language, duh."

AMY: It's astonishing to think of how our story is now intertwined. So much is different about our families, and yet the common theme is our immigrant history: our families leaving behind strife, war, and poverty for the hope of freedom and a better future in America. I am the first person in my family to be born in the United States—my parents and my older sister were among the big wave of Korean immigrants who came to America in the 1970s. My parents grew up in the Korean War and its aftermath. It's hard to remember now, but Korea was one of the poorest countries in the world in the fifties and sixties and was on the brink of humanitarian crises. Rebecca's grandparents fled Nazi-occupied Europe in order to save their future generations, but I grew up eating kimchi in Chicago. Rebecca grew up eating pupusas on Shabbat in Los Angeles. Our grandparents literally would have never had the opportunity to lay eyes on each other. They wouldn't have had any common language to even speak to each other. And now Rebecca and I call the very same place home. My six words on my family's story: "Where am I *from*? Chicago. Suburbs."

REBECCA: I lived in Europe in 2003 during the beginning of the Iraq War. I was constantly told, "Oh, you're not American, you're European," as if it were a compliment. I would fervently answer, "No, I am American. I would not exist if it weren't for America. My story is the American story." Immigrants are always the most pro-America.

AMY: The beauty of it is that the American story is always shifting. It's not always easy—there are inherent tensions to living in a culture that is always changing, and inherent challenges to being new to a culture that isn't always the most accommodating. I mean, how many times can a lady be asked where she's *really* from? But that challenge is also invigorating for first- and second-generation immigrants. How do we make choices and lives that honor our roots while creating new traditions and cultures? How do we live on the hyphen and celebrate it?

REBECCA: We've come full circle from trying to assimilate into the mainstream culture to shaping what culture is in America. Ultimately, it's our American ability to adapt and absorb and to transform ourselves that makes us *us*. It's what we *love* about America. It's what makes our lives so rich.

Sí, there are Jews
from Argentina.

—Juan Diego Gerscovich

Nobody believed this blond was Mexican.

—Gyl Grinberg

Soccer: cheer "USA!" *and* "¡Viva México!"

—Ari (age 15), Max (age 13), and Isabella (age 5) Grinberg

REVOLUTION. DECLARATION.
IMMIGRATION. INSPIRATION.
MIGHTY NATION!

—Jan Kreuzer

Mom thought American soldier was cute.

—Anne Kennedy

Made in Havana.
Born in Miami.

—Marlene Braga

Five-year-old watches Disney,
names herself Alice.

—Alice Lu

Hillbilly by birth, European by DNA.

—Andy Greene

Russian pogroms,
time to bounce, y'all.

—Amanda Hamilton

Six months old:
First passport stamp.

—Xander Greene (age 11)

**Past: Raped.
Immigrated. Spoke out. Out.**

—Cristhian P.

Neither here nor there: survivor history.

—Francis C. Madi-Cerrada

Unemployed Québécoise crossed
illegally, nobody cared.

—Morgan Morrissette

IRISH GRANDMOTHER,
AGE NINE, SENT ALONE.

—Margaret Mackin

JAMAICAN CANADIAN NEUROSCIENTIST
FINDS FOREVER HOME.

—Ayanna Bryan

The Enemy of Indoctrination Is Exposure

By Zak Ebrahim

On November 5, 1990, when I was seven years old, my father assassinated the extremist Rabbi Meir Kahane in New York City. From his prison cell my father was then sentenced to life in prison, along with the men involved in the 1993 World Trade Center bombing, for attempting to orchestrate a plot to bomb a dozen New York City landmarks. I have spent much of my life trying to understand the path that led my father to abandon his family—a loving wife and three children—for an ideology that preached hatred of those who did not fit into his narrow worldview.

Fear and isolation are two of the most important ingredients in radicalization. I believe these are the forces that drove my father into the arms of fanatics, and part of the foundation he used to indoctrinate me into his worldview. I can say unequivocally that it was exposure to those I was taught to hate that brought me out of this ideology. The first time I made a Jewish friend or a gay friend, the stereotypes I had been taught were forcibly contrasted with real-life experience. Those relationships were the ones that first planted the seed in my mind that perhaps what I had been taught was a lie.

One of the great strengths of our country is that we are a melting pot. Yes, we are Americans, but what is America if not an amalgamation of countless languages, cultures, religions, and people from all over the world? To be an American is to have a willingness to forge a path where one has not yet traveled. Without being exposed to different ideologies and cultures, I never would have been able to escape my indoctrination. It is the melting pot that saved me. That is why I share my own story publicly. Where I come from is complex and upsetting. But what I have learned as I chose to speak about the power of peace is simple: our diversity makes us stronger.

Zak Ebrahim is the author of The Terrorist's Son: A Story of Choice.

I am not
my country's past.

—Lindley McCutcheon (age 14)

American soul grounded
by Haitian roots.

—Robinson Vil

First grade decision:
lose French accent.

—Péralte Paul

The simple Australian life
turned supersize.

—Jasmine Grace

Indian Muslim southerner
who says "y'all."

—Shaheen Rana

FROM COLOMBIA TO COLUMBIA:
27 YEARS.

—Marissa Catalina Casey

"You will be notified; be patient."

—Duan Fangming

Brought by force,
stayed with intention.

—Adam Brown

Egyptian graduate student meets
Mayflower descendant.

—Adel Assaad

Grandmother's ashes.
My mother rises, flies.

—Shanthi Sekaran

Two cultures, two languages,
four generations.

—Win Mui

ARMY MAN MET PANAMANIAN
BUILDING CANAL.

—Travis Pringle

Twenty years on a visa,
waiting.

—Freb Hunt-Bull

"Why you no get straight A's?"

—Regina Soo

An American girl outside, refugee inside.

—Sabrina Fedel

Germany. Catherine. Russia.
Bolshevik rebellion. America.

—K. L. Engelman

Illustrated by Hazel Santino

Vaffanculo, Catholic Church—Hello, Los Angeles!

—Hazel Santino, on her grandfather's
six words upon moving from Italy to America.

Was a Refugee, Now a Restaurateur

By Exion Huynh

My parents were refugees from the Vietnam War. They survived hardships and experienced unimaginable things. My father was a South Vietnamese soldier and told me war stories about how he survived being shot six times, once in the head and face. He had fake teeth and scars; it's amazing he survived.

My parents endured the boat trip to Malaysia and were eventually rescued and sent to the US. My mother had a necklace that she sold for $25. They spent that money at Pizza Hut. They ended up working at a Chinese restaurant in Little Rock, Arkansas, and then started their own restaurant. The *Fresh Off the Boat* show parallels my life, as I grew up working in a restaurant and struggling to find my place at school from the late eighties to nineties. I joined the navy in 1998 after finishing high school, and my parents opened up two more restaurants before they finally retired in the year 2000.

Exion Huynh is a US Navy hospital corpsman stationed at Camp Pendleton in California.

Learned English in a restaurant kitchen.

—Rémi Granger

Moved, moved, moved, moved, moved, moved.

—Anna Sanders (age 15)

Left as something,
arrived as nothing.

—Henry Feldman

SHALLOW ROOTS,
I FEEL TIPPY EVERYWHERE.

—Paolo Marchesi

"Mogadishu Columbus"=
safe shelter from warlords.

—Adbi-Hakim Mohamed

**Safe, but still always
feeling lonely.**

—Martin D. OCampo

Behind the Number, Visa, Papers: Person

By Doreen Kindler

I'm one of 240,000 plus people who serve the American public as employees of the Department of Homeland Security. Our mission: "With honor and integrity, we will safeguard the American people, our homeland, and our values."

Most of us are drawn to this work because of personal experience: military service, law enforcement background, or our passion for working in the international realm. For me, it was growing up as the child of immigrants, being multilingual, studying international relations, and then working in higher education as an international affairs administrator for twenty years. I worked with thousands of international students coming to the United States and facilitated study abroad for thousands more to head out from here to destinations around the world.

Now I provide immigration expertise and training to support schools that enroll international students, which in turn helps students maintain their legal status; the schools I work with enroll tens of thousands of students of the more than one million total in the United States each year. International educational exchange is soft diplomacy; it makes the world a smaller place. As I counsel schools on how to advise their students to maintain their status, I always remember that behind the number, the visa, the legal papers, there is a person with hopes, dreams, and goals for their future—maybe even a future world leader.

Doreen Kindler works for the Department of Homeland Security.

Photo by Shauna Greene's iPhone

NATURALIZED CITIZENS. PROUDLY CALL AMERICA HOME.

–**Mon** and **Nabin Chhetri**, on March 7, 2017, as the couple were sworn in as naturalized US citizens under the gold dome of the Georgia State Capitol. International Rescue Committee in Atlanta assisted them through the application process.

Summer:
read entire US history textbook.

—J. Abby

What is the
Mayflower Compact

$10,800

"Jeopardy!" courtesy Jeopardy Productions, Inc.

Land of opportunity lets me learn.

—Sharath Narayan, winner of *Jeopardy!* Teen Tournament

**Learning about cultures
awakens your spirit.**

—Claudia Fitzwater

Somebody helped me, now my turn.

–Nadia Kasvin

Grandson of four immigrants. Worried American.

–David Gaboardi

100% Korean; 100% white; 2% milk.

–Julian Lee-Zacheis

American while working, Peruvian while parenting.

–Osualdo Leon

Home: anywhere they let you in.

–Janet Kirchheimer

"Hear the one about the Iranian-American?"

By Maz Jobrani

Photo by Justin Baker

I was one of the founding members of the Axis of Evil Comedy Tour. The other founding members were Ahmed Ahmed, an Egyptian-American, and Aron Kader, a Palestinian-American. And then there was me, the Iranian-American of the group. Being Iranian-American presents its own set of problems. Those two countries haven't gotten along lately, so it causes a lot of inner conflict: part of me likes me, part of me hates me. Part of me thinks I should have a nuclear program, the other part thinks I can't be trusted with one. These are dilemmas an Iranian-American has every day.

I was born in Iran; I'm now an American citizen, with an American passport, which means I can travel outside the United States. Although given Trump's policies I may not be able to come back! Still, if you only have an Iranian passport, you're kind of limited to the countries you can go to with open arms, you know—Syria, Venezuela, North Korea.

As anyone who's gotten his passport in America will tell you, it still indicates what country you were born in. I remember getting my American passport. I was like, "Woo-hoo! I'm going to travel." And I opened it up, it said, BORN IN IRAN. I'm like, "Oh, come on, man!"

> **Getting my American passport, I was like, "Woo-hoo! I'm going to travel." And I opened it up, it said, "Born in Iran." I'm like, "Oh, come on, man!"**

I've actually never had trouble in any Western countries with my American passport, even though it says, BORN IN IRAN. No problems. Where I've had problems is in some of the Arab countries. I guess some of the Arab countries aren't getting along with Iran either. I was in Kuwait recently, doing a comedy show with some other American comedians. They all went through. Then the border patrol saw my American passport: "Ah-ha! American, great." Then he opened it up. "Born in Iran? Wait."

He started asking me questions. He said: "What is your father's name?" I said, "Well, he passed away, but his name was Khosro." He said: "What is your grandfather's name?" I said: "He passed away a long time ago. His name was Jabbar." He said: "You wait. I'll be back," and he walked away. I started freaking out, because I don't know what kind of crap my grandfather was into. I thought the guy was going to come back and be like, "We've been looking for you for two hundred years. Your grandfather has a parking violation. It's way overdue. You owe us two billion dollars."

I actually speak with an American accent, so you would think, as an Iranian-American actor, I should be able to play any part: good, bad, what have you. But a lot of times in Hollywood, when casting directors find out you're of Middle Eastern descent, they say, "Oh, you're Iranian. Great! Can you say, 'I will kill you in the name of Allah?'" I respond, "I could say that, but what if I were to say, 'Hello. I'm your doctor'?" They go, "Great! And then you blow up the hospital."

So one thing I try to do with my stand-up is break stereotypes. And I've been guilty of stereotyping as well. A few years ago I was in Dubai, a place where lots of Indians work, and many don't get paid that well. So I got it in my head that all the Indians must be workers. I forgot there are obviously successful Indians in Dubai, too. I was doing a show, and the club owner said, "We'll send a driver to pick you up." I went down to the lobby, and saw this Indian guy. He's standing there in a cheap suit, thin mustache, staring at me, so I figure he must be my driver. "Excuse me," I say, "are you my driver?" "No, sir," he replied. "I own the hotel."

"I'm sorry!" I said. "But why were you staring at me?"

"Well, I thought you were my driver."

Maz Jobrani is the author of I'm Not a Terrorist But I've Played One on TV *and costar of the sitcom* Superior Donuts. *He has had three Showtime stand-up comedy specials, and performs stand-up live around the world, including the Middle East, where he performed in front of the king of Jordan.*

HEADSCARF CHANGED HOW PEOPLE TREATED ME.

—Amani Al-Khatahtbeh

Russian immigrant learns English, becomes MD.

–Nataliya Garrison

Years later I landed in English.

—Julia Alvarez

Dominican gypsy with
New York soul.

—Laura Gomez

South American rhythms,
North American style.

—Kieran Cabezas

NO, NOT RELATED TO MILEY. PERSIAN.

—Niki Cyrus

Peanut butter spread
in pita bread.

—Jessica Elsayed

Four immigrant grandparents.
One American family.

—Greg Wachtenheim

Daughters' sweat equity
paid son's tuition.

—Lisa Carlson

Played clarinet
in lieu of tickets.

—Kristen Pachl Malachowski

He didn't get on the *Titanic*

—Roby Marcou

From Ireland to NY,
served Roosevelts.

—Steven J. Dermody

Waiting for the Disneyland
Wajahat keychain.

—Wajahat Ali

Photo by Larry Smith's iPhone

I CAN'T SPELL MY GRANDMOTHER'S NAME.

—Matthew Foster Walsh

Enslaved. No escape.
Fingernails clawed ships.

–Van Garrett

"Wait, how do you pronounce that?"

–Lori Der Sahakian (age 15)

PASSAGE WASN'T MIDDLE, ONLY THE BEGINNING.

–Morgan Tucker

Risen above Jim Crow. Keep rising.

–Eric "Ricky" McKinnie, Blind Boys of Alabama

SHE "VANTED" TO BE A YANKEE.

–Dyan Titchnell

Long Chinese story.
American: short, sweet.

—Lili Liu

I KNOW MY GREAT-GRANDDAD FROM WIKIPEDIA.

—Julian Pearson Rickenbach

Out of potatoes? Time to leave.

—Sam Coates

Burger for lunch,
curry for dinner.

—Saji Philip

GRANDPA WORKS HARD,
EARNS GRANDMA'S PASSAGE.

—Phyllis Fulton

I'm Afro-Latino. Always Latino, always Black.

—Juan Robles

FOREIGN ACCENT: a SIGN OF BRAVERY.

—Amy Chua

Korean grandparents, Korean parents, American me.

—Joon Cho

"SO, LIKE, WHAT ARE WE?" HUMANS.

—Noel Anaya

Politically borderless world belongs to everyone.

—Tara Dhungana

They Farmed for Interned Japanese Neighbors

By Ellis Reyes

My grandparents were immigrants from the Philippines. They and many other families in central California kept their Japanese neighbors' farms up and running while they were interned during World War II. When these families returned home, they were able to pick up where they had left off before their imprisonment. These acts of humanity have led to family friendships that now span four generations.

Ellis Reyes is a middle school teacher in the Seattle area.

Immigrants have always made America great.

—Pedro Noguera

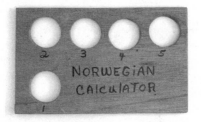

GRANDMOTHER MADE HER OWN GAG GIFTS.

—Robert Odegard

I feel more American than Indian.

—Zaynah Ahmed

American in Korea. Korean in America.

—Louis Choy

Immigrant. Worker. Sole provider. Extraordinary woman.

—Jackie Childress

Google Translate is my other language.

—Diohan Goncalves (age 17)

Forks at school, chopsticks at home.

—Eva Ting

Even Siri does not understand me.

—Dafna DeBasc Levis

"What do you mean, you're Hmong?"

—Pang Foua Melchor

From melting pot, multicultural Thanksgiving meals.

—Maria Vickroy-Peralta

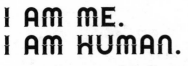

I AM ME.
I AM HUMAN.

—Gene Simmons

Lost Alps. Found Rockies.
Kept Freud.

—George L. Mizner

**Fought Nazis,
then Communists.
Refugee family.**

—Stephanie Bogdanich

*Queer Latino dancing through
intersectional rhythms.*

—Roberto Carlos Ortiz

Bottom of slave ship to Virginia.

—Tyeast Pettit

An egg: white outside,
yellow inside.

—Miles Bishop

"Help wanted.
No Irish need apply."

—Liz McGlinchey King

Illegal immigrant, but in the 1900s.

—Alex Caligiuri

Vikings, Lenape Indians,
Quakers, Pilgrims. Us.

—Susanna French

Byproducts of war: scientist,
professor, doctor.

—Truc HaMai

Tough living with livestock
in Holland.

—Jon Vanderbeek

Child Alone, Judge Smiles, Child Shakes

By Lenni Benson

Between October 2014 and October 2016, nearly one hundred thousand unaccompanied children were apprehended at the southern United States/Mexico border and taken into federal custody. All children are placed into removal proceedings; Mexican children, however, are more often than not simply pushed back at the border. New York receives a high percentage of these children, and the New York City Immigration Court has nearly fifteen thousand juvenile cases out of the court's workload of seventy-five thousand immigration cases.

These six-word impressions are based on my work with pro bono attorneys and immigrant youth since 2006. The children describe the journey, the arrival at the United States border, and their hopes.

Deportation Hearing
Child alone,
Judge smiles,
Child shakes.

Crossing the River
Smuggler points,
Border guard beckons,
Detained.

La Bestia (the Train)
Leap, grab,
Pray, cling,
Leap, freedom.

The Choice When the Gang Comes
You join
Or you
Die; flee.

Picture of Home in El Salvador
Age 8,
Draws house,
Bars everywhere.

"Not Dangerous"
Guns, knives, death;
Not dangerous, normal.

Juvenile Docket in Immigration Court
Attorney gasps:
"WTF,
Not in America."

Lenni Benson is the founder of the Safe Passage Project (https://www.safepassageproject.org/), a nonprofit seeking to ensure no child faces deportation alone.

Six-Word Memoirs staff visited a number of ESL classes across the country and invited folks to share their (often recent) immigration stories, challenging students to express themselves in their second (or third!) language. Here we share just a few of the many impressions we heard from these brave language learners on coming to America.

Photo courtesy of Amy Rothberger

Love French fries, miss Yemeni kabsa.

—Dawlah Ali

I, TOO, SING AMERICA AND YEMEN.

—Mlyon Almasoodi

I want to know my rights.

—Sanaa Nagi

Through the storm to
safer waters.

—Steve Snyder

*I like the freedom
in America.*

—Yu Ci Lei

Old ways won't open new doors.

—Mariya Voronchak

**I'm happy;
I like America's flowers.**

—Zhong Yan Jiang

Saw Bubby's Name at Ellis Island

By Elisa Shevitz

Photo by Alvin Shevitz

Most of the relatives on my mom's side arrived at Baltimore Inner Harbor, so I was surprised when my dad told me his mother had arrived in America through Ellis Island. My dad had wanted to see the new Ellis Island museum, but there never seemed to be time during their visits to see me in New York City, where I had lived my whole adult life.

Usually when my parents spent the weekend with me, it was for a specific reason, and we'd run around like crazy: an antiques show at the pier, a birthday celebration, the theater. One summer weekend, when they were in town and we finally had nothing planned, we decided to take a ferry to Ellis Island—a place that somehow none of us had ever been to before. It was an exquisitely beautiful day, and for some reason I had my camera with me (before iPhones) and took lots of shots of us laughing and posing with the Statue of Liberty in the background.

While ostensibly the point of our voyage was a ferry ride, it was the museum that was most memorable. Seeing my bubby's name, Jeanne Flitman, even just in a searchable archive, gave me goose bumps. My dad and I proudly stood where she may have stood as a little girl with her mother (Esther, who I'm named after), having been sent for by her father, who had come ahead to run a hotel in Baltimore.

The day we were there was on a weekend in August 2001. Later, looking through my photos the next month, I saw the twin towers of the World Trade Center framing many of the shots. I couldn't believe I had captured those images so vividly. The contrast was chilling: stories of new beginnings filling the archives of the museum juxtaposed against the tragic ending that would take the lives of so many.

Elisa Shevitz is a writer living in New York City.

PROTECTING HUMAN RIGHTS—OUR NATION'S FOUNDATION.

–The Honorable Jimmy Carter, thirty-ninth president of the United States

Escaped Odessa.
Holocaust.
Great-granddaughter
named Odessa.

—Tiffany Shlain

So proud to be
a Zuidgeest.

—Ginger Zee

DANCE CARD FILLED WITH
UNPRONOUNCEABLE NAMES.

—Amy Rothberger

Photo by Alessandra Wollner

I am a fifteenth generation immigrant.

—Susan Eddins

Big dreams, big extremes, big sandwiches.

—Suzy Barnard

Even the air smells different here.

—Emilie Schwarz

Can't touch her on my phone.

—Yawen Yu (age 17)

Descended from Nazis. Now American leftist.

—Dylan Brown

Thicker Aussie accent gets better tips.

—Yael Stone

HINDU AND INDIAN ARE NOT LANGUAGES.

—Chetan Vadali (age 15)

Fare bella figura (Don't embarrass me!)

—Anthony Giglio

Teenager arrives alone from czarist Russia.

—Karen Haskin

Grandfather Yitzhak Dymant became Jack Diamond.

—Jeff Tiedrich

Rebuilt lives following the Armenian genocide.

—Cathy Pohan

NOBODY IS EVER JUST A REFUGEE.

—Chimamanda Ngozi Adichie

Thrice MIGrant.
HARvesting the story, ALwAys.

–Kiran Singh Sirah

From banana republic
to concrete jungle.

–Mayra Aldás-Deckert

came early to farm. Kept farming.

–Helen Husher

Grandma immigrated
at ten to work.

–Lori Wells

HADN'T TWO PENNETH OF COLD GIN.

–Ivor Julius Silver

Photo courtesy of Nava family

OUR GRANDPARENTS DID
SO WE COULD.

—Alejandro Brown (bottom right),
with Papa Leyva and his ten grandchildren

No, I do not speak "Indian."

—Esha Chadha

Chinese women look
at me expectantly.

—Emily Chung

**North Dakota
winter beats Russian
pogroms.**

—Jessica Berlin

**Life's better here with
wheelchair access.**

—Brenda Gonzalez

BEGAN AS LABORERS, LATER
ENDOWED MUSEUM.

—Ellen Spertus

Photo by Larry Smith's iPhone

I do not know kung fu.

—David L. (age 13)

IMMIGRANTS, WE GET THE JOB DONE.

—Lin-Manuel Miranda, *Hamilton*

Welcome to America;
please don't leave.

—Lily T. (age 11)

Centimeter by centimeter,
foot by foot.

—L. G. Smith

The best is yet to come.

—Mark Cuban

WE'RE ALL IN THE SAME BOAT,

—Eldon Asp

I dreamed.
I made it happen.

—Prabal Gurung

Acknowledgments

"Many hands have kept me afloat." I borrow these six words from the writer Nick Flynn, shared in the very first book of Six-Word Memoirs. There are so many people who have made the Six-Word Memoir project shine, and this new book has been the most collaborative effort to date. Special thanks to Shauna Healy Greene, who wakes up as obsessed by the power of this short form of storytelling as anyone I've worked with, and once again has been an invaluable editor. Amy Rothberger and Alessandra Wollner are both terrific editors and excellent story seekers, taking deep dives as they engaged storytellers in classrooms, community centers, protest marches, and more. More than six words of appreciation go out to community manager Jonathan Zipper, as well as interns Zaynah Ahmed, Paige Brown, and Amanda Gaglione. Wendy Lefkon, Laura Hopper, and the team at Kingswell have been a joy to work with as we put together a puzzle with many pieces, as has my unflappable agent David Patterson. Steven Melnick, head of marketing for 20th Century Fox Television (the studio behind *Fresh Off the Boat*), first approached me with the idea of working with the show and has been this book's obsessed champion and invaluable adviser. My wife, Piper Kerman, is my best editor and nonstop source of care and counsel in every part of my life. Our son keeps me on my toes, and watching his fingers count to "six" as he writes his own six-word stories is as good as it gets.

Thank you to the many partners and collaborators who shared this project with their communities and constituents. From refugee resettlement agencies and English language schools to immigrant rights organizations and youth programs, you brought Six-Word Memoirs to new audiences. Below is a list of many of the groups who we were fortunate to work with; and I'd like to send a special shout-out to ACLU advocacy and policy counsel Jonathan Blazer, as well as my sister, Susie Smith, for connecting us. What follows is by no means a comprehensive list of all the organizations doing great work in the field of immigration, simply the handful that helped make this book possible. —**Larry Smith**

Collaborators

826 Valencia is dedicated to supporting under-resourced students ages six to eighteen with their creative and expository writing skills and to helping teachers inspire their students to write. *826valencia.org*

The **ACLU** (American Civil Liberties Union) Immigrants' Rights Project is dedicated to expanding and enforcing the civil liberties and civil rights of immigrants, and combating public and private discrimination against them. *aclu.org/issues/immigrants-rights*

The **Arab American Association of New York** works to support and empower the Arab immigrant and Arab American communities by providing services to help them adjust to their new home and become active members of society. *arabamericanny.org*

The **Chinese Progressive Association** works towards social and economic justice in New York City's Chinatown and Lower East Side communities through education, advocacy, service, and organizing programs. *cpanyc.weebly.com*

Photo by Callum Bondy

Community Refugee and Immigration Services (CRIS) works to help refugees and immigrants reach and sustain self-sufficiency and achieve successful integration into the central Ohio community. *crisohio.org*

Immigration Equality is the nation's leading LGBTQ immigration rights organization, advocating for and representing lesbian, gay, bisexual, transgender, queer (LGBTQ), and HIV-positive immigrants seeking safety, fair treatment, and freedom. *immigrationequality.org*

You build walls, we build ladders.
—Alexis Miramontes, 17

The **International Rescue Committee** responds to the world's worst humanitarian crises and helps people whose lives and livelihoods are shattered by conflict and disaster to survive, recover, and gain control of their future. *rescue.org*

ICNA Relief Chicago works on various social-service projects to strengthen communities and families in need as an expression of the teachings of Islam. ICNA Relief Chicago's services are primarily in the areas of disaster response and relief, transitional housing, and refugee empowerment. *icnachicago.org/projects/icna-relief*

The **Karam Foundation** develops innovative education programs for Syrian refugee youth, distributes smart aid to Syrian families, and funds sustainable development projects initiated by Syrians for Syrians. *karamfoundation.org*

The **New York Immigration Coalition** represents the collective interests of New York's diverse immigrant communities and devises solutions to advance them, advocating for laws, policies, and programs that lead to justice and opportunity for all immigrant groups. *thenyic.org*

Youth Radio is an outlet for Bay Area youth to process their experiences and provide an alternative perspective to the prevailing media dialogue and transform an under-invested part of Oakland, California, into a world-class center of art, commerce, and culture. *youthradio.org*

Photo by Steve Melnick

Fresh Off the Boat's cast and crew in Taipei, Taiwan, the setting for the "Coming from America" episode about the Huang family visiting the parents' birthplace.